MESSA

The Photographs of Emma D. Sewall 1836–1919

MESSAGE THROUGH TIME

The Photographs of Emma D. Sewall 1836–1919

ABBIE SEWALL

THE HARPSWELL PRESS, *Gardiner, Maine*

Excerpt from *String Too Short To Be Saved* by Donald Hall. Copyright 1979 by Donald Hall. Reprinted by permission of David R. Godine, Publisher, Boston Massachusetts

Excerpts from *The World of Atget* by Berenice Abbott. Copyright 1964 by Berenice Abbott. Reprinted by permission of the author.

FIRST EDITION

Library of Congress Catalog Card Number: 88–83765
ISBN 0–88448–059–3 Cloth
0–88448–058–5 Paper
0–88448–057–7 Deluxe Limited

Designed on Crummett Mountain by Edith Allard
Typography, printing and binding by Meriden-Stinehour Press, Lunenburg, Vermont

The Harpswell Press
The Boston Building
132 Water Street
Gardiner, Maine 04345

Manufactured in the United States of America

TO MY CHILDREN
Emily and Thatcher

Acknowledgements

Without continued help and support from many people, this book could not have been completed. First and foremost, I am forever grateful to my publisher, Logan Johnston, for his belief in me and Emma, and to my husband, Rob Shultz, for his support and patience during the years I have worked on the project. Bill Pohl, with whom I coauthored *The Voice of Maine*, pushed me to proceed before I had the confidence to do so. Earle (Bud) Warren, a maritime and Bath historian, saw Emma's photographs very early in the project, and his excitement propelled me. My parents, Bill and Phebe Sewall, and my aunt, Mary Hyde, let me explore family attics. Mary Hyde and Nicholas and Jean Sewall lent me Emma's original photographs to copy so I could make my own negative file of her work. Other family members, such as the late Dorothy Sewall Jayne and Mrs. Arthur Sewall II, consented to interviews, even though I often didn't know the right questions to ask. I also interviewed Mrs. John Lasell and Mrs. Loyall Sewall, both of whom took an active interest in the project. Every time a friend or relative asked about the project, they raised more questions, which ultimately helped direct me in uncovering the mysteries surrounding Emma's life.

Tom Jones of Brunswick allowed me to use his sophisticated copy camera to photograph Emma's original work and John McKee of Bowdoin College critiqued my prints. John W. Coffey, former curator of the Bowdoin College Museum of Art, gave support, became a friend, and made valuable suggestions. Alan Johanson of Atlanta shared his expertise on antiquated photographic equipment and processes. Tom Davies of Philadelphia shared his information on the platinum printing process.

Thanks also go to Max Dawson of Bath, whose assistance was crucial to the completion of this book.

In researching Emma's life, I discovered the difficulties involved in collecting data from many different sources when no information has previously been gathered. Estelle Jussim, photo-historian and author of the award-winning *Slave To Beauty*, advised me on how to stick to the task at hand without getting distracted by every tangent that would invariably crop up. Cynthia English at the Boston Athenaeum guided me in my research of the Boston Camera Club. Margo Galacar of the Ipswich Historical Society lent me her archives on the Ipswich Female Seminary. Gordan Struble of the Patten Free Library in Bath taught me how to use historical reference books, antiquated newspapers, microfilm, and genealogical sources. Mrs. Richard Alden of New Harbor allowed me to spend many, many hours at her dining-room table copying information out of a Sewall genealogy book. Dr. Alfred Holt also shared his work on Sewall genealogy and helped resolve some mix-ups way back in the Sewall line. Barbara Hastings of Woolwich shared her information on the Crooker family and genealogy, as did Mrs. Harriet C. Hill and her son Richard S. Hill of Bath.

Thanks also go to Everett Murchie of Fitchburg, Massachusetts, for his information on Fitchburg's Postal Photographic Club. He was the only source outside the now-rare *American Amateur Photographer* periodicals that produced any explanation of this long-extinct organization.

At the Maine Maritime Museum in Bath, Nathan Lipfert offered tireless assistance over the years in researching the Sewall family archives. It was also Nathan who suggested turning the project into a slide show and lecture for the Maritime Museum, which quickly blossomed into more slide shows and lectures for other groups. Through this format I learned how to make slides from photographs, how to become a better writer, and how to speak in front of an audience. I am grateful for all of these acquired skills.

How can I begin to thank the five intelligent, sensitive women who assisted me through the various stages of writing this book? Emily Herman, Manli Ho, Susan Ransom, my sister Laura, and Liz Pierson all edited and re-edited my writing. They lovingly added layer upon layer to my understanding of how to write what you feel—and what you mean.

I am also deeply indebted to many people I haven't mentioned here who indirectly helped keep the project afloat by enriching my life through friendship and support. Also, my daughter Emily and son Thatcher deserve tremendous credit for their patience and resourcefulness when I was in the darkroom or using the computer. For as long as they both have been alive, I've worked on one book and then another.

I also want to thank Emmie Wyman of Phippsburg, the last person I interviewed. At ninety-eight, she is still very sharp and can remember subtle nuances about the times Emma photographed her as a child. For her, each photograph had a story. I could almost see the wheels of time turning backward in her mind as she carefully devoured every detail of every image I placed before her. Many times she let out a gasp of recognition and pleasure, followed by reminiscences from her childhood. My interview with her gave me an experience I'll never forget for I watched Emma's photographs work their message *backwards* through time with the same impact they had worked *forward* in time with me.

MESSAGE THROUGH TIME

The Photographs of Emma D. Sewall 1836–1919

I believe the photographer's eye develops to a more intense awareness than other people's, as a dancer develops his muscles and limbs, and a musician his ear. . . . The photographer's act is to see the outside world precisely, with intelligence as well as sensuous insight. The act of seeing sharpens the eye to an unprecedented acuteness. He often sees swiftly an entire scene that most people would pass unnoticed. His vision is objective, primarily. His focus is on the world, the scene, the subject, the detail. As he scans his subject he sees as the lens sees, which differs from human vision. Simultaneously he sees the end result, which is to say he sees photographically.

Berenice Abbott

Introduction

T*his is Emma Sewall's book*, even though she lived over a century ago and did not write it. Emma was a remarkable woman who quietly took on the photographic art world when it was just beginning to bloom, quickly made a name for herself in this country and in Paris, and then just as quietly slipped from view.

Emma had an eye for the dramatic. Just look at *When the Day's Work is Done* or *Fording the River.* The first time I saw her photographs, I was a timid girl of fifteen. Yet I knew instantly, with total conviction, that Emma's ability to transform the ordinary into the dramatic, to convey universality and dignity in her subject matter, was a reflection of an extraordinary spirit. In that first moment, I also knew that Emma was making a dramatic connection with me, her great-great-granddaughter, across five generations of time.

My belief in the power of her photographs has never wavered. In fact, as my photographic vision became more sophisticated with age, I was able to appreciate Emma's photographs more deeply. Studying photography, while constantly referring back to Emma's work, gave me a certain standard of vision which strongly influenced my own photography and reaffirmed my initial conviction in hers. From a historical perspective the importance of Emma's photographs is obvious as we slip further and further from the simple value of physical labor which contributed to the growth of the country. Nontheless, the recognition Emma received in her own time confirms that her work easily stands on its own. The purity of her vision was apparent then as it is now.

What is remarkable is that Emma's subjects are not sensational, but are nonetheless moving in their familiarity, their unadorned realism. The subjects appear so real, so immediate, that they almost leave the flat surface of the photograph to take on a three-dimensional, lifelike quality. The photographer's presence does not interfere with the subject seen through the camera lens. This immediate directness and familiarity in each vignette conveys a sense of continuity between past and present, and in this way a connection between people is made.

Emma was shy and reserved, at times reclusive, yet never passive. Emma personified Thomas Merton's philosophy when he said, "Our real journey is interior. A matter of growth, deepening, and surrender to the creative action of love and grace in our hearts." Emma's independent thinking was her driving force; she was shaped by this more than any single event in her life. Intense devotion to intellectual and philosophical clarification steered her to a life of the mind. It was the way she thought about things—the deliberate integration of formal education with her strong female sensitivity and pioneering spirit—that informed the artist-photographer. Photography gave Emma license to explore the values and insights acquired by her inquisitive mind. She was unafraid, even proud, to draw from all these parts of herself in her search for the common thread, the unifying theme. This inner-directed thought gave her a way to step out of herself, and the cultural assumptions about her class and sex, to empower her photographs. By defying social boundaries of what was possible, she far exceeded the expectations of women in her day.

The choice of photography seems natural to Emma's way of thinking. Berenice Abbott has said, "Every step in the process of making a photograph is preceded by a conscious decision which depends on the man in back of the camera and the qualities that go to make up that man, his taste, to say nothing of his philosophy."

Emma joins the list of more well known photographers from the turn of the century who used the medium for personal search. F. Holland Day, Alfred Stieglitz, and Alvin Langdon Coburn, among others, possessed attitudes deviant from their tradition. European art, the study of history and literature, and a rising interest in the occult became artistic forces at work in the collective mind of American photographers. The dawn of the machine age and the expanding roles of women as more women became educated and went to work were but two of the enormous cultural forces that were also changing the social climate and challenging spiritual values of Emma's day.

Photography was Emma's passion, the culminating medium of her life, the medium by which she could put everything she thought and felt into an expressive form. Because her discovery of this creative outlet came so late in life, every moment was precious. This is partially what elevated her energy and commitment to the level of passion. Outside photography, Emma was the antithesis of passion, a controlled woman of proper social standing and etiquette.

At the time I began my work to reveal Emma's identity and share her photographs, I had no idea that I would be embarking on a rich journey of self-discovery. The benefits of these new awarenesses will affect me for the rest of my life. Specifically, Emma kindled my own interest in photography, which resulted in a career of photojournalism. Also, knowledge of Emma showed me who I am by revealing where I came from. She has given me my place in the world through the continuum of family, and in a larger sense evolution, by personalizing my history and defining my female roots.

Like so many women in history, Emma and her accomplishments were quickly forgotten, even by her family. With very little documentation of her life, and an obituary that tells nothing more than who her father, husband, and sons were, many gaps remain. The largest missing ingredient is a diary or journal, which women of her era and background commonly kept. Writings by Emma that have survived clearly suggest a well-practiced hand. Her book, *The*

Rivers and Marshes of Small Point, her letters to her husband, Arthur, and the diary calendar she created for her son, William, all convey the eloquence of style, confidence, and sensitivity of someone who wrote often and well. I feel certain that Emma did keep a journal. Is it still lying forgotten or lost in some dusty corner? Or did she deliberately destroy it before she died? Given her obsessive need of privacy, especially in later years, and her awareness of the photographic legacy she would be leaving for future generations, the latter seems quite possible. Her photographs, however, are what ultimately reveal who Emma was, more than the facts or the missing facts of her life. It was her photographs that made such a tremendous impression on me; through her clarity of vision I glimpsed her exceptional quality of mind.

While researching Emma's life, I discovered that there are many women scholars (with lettered degrees) devoting their lives to rescuing women obscured by time and history. They, too, have scant information to go by. They, too, are discovering role models out of the creative works and legacies left behind by long-forgotten women. And these scholars are setting down in writing a new kind of biography and history—a blending of heart and mind, a history less dry, more human. In this way our collective history is being enriched with a more complete picture of the past. As women's roles evolve and expand, it becomes ever more important that we all have access to our female heritage and to the wisdom and experience of women who came before us.

Emma was the first to show me, at the impressionable age of fifteen, that women can have an impact on the world by what they think and create. This became clear with the powerful and immediate impact I felt when I first saw her photographs. It was as if her images and their meaning, and the power of photography, were permanently imprinted in my psyche as an example of how I could live and make a difference. Nothing since that moment has hit me in the same way, nor has anything affected the direction of my life so profoundly. I believe it was one of those things a person may experience once, maybe twice, in a lifetime.

Now, twenty years after my first encounter with Emma's work, I still believe she left a message for me, and the world at large, in her photographs. Her message is that we are all connected. Generation after generation, we are the same despite our differences. I can see it in the faces of her subjects, their expressions and mannerisms. They are people seriously engaged in the business of working and living, as we are, generation after generation. Her photographs celebrate life then and now. The beauty of her photographs is in the eloquence and grace with which Emma imparted this information.

Message Through Time is a homage to an extraordinary early photographer, my spiritual mentor and role model. With great pleasure, I offer her message to you.

Abbie Sewall
Bath, Maine
December 7, 1988

To be without a history is like being forgotten. My grandfather did not know the maiden names of either of his grandmothers. I thought that to be forgotten must be the worst fate of all.

Donald Hall

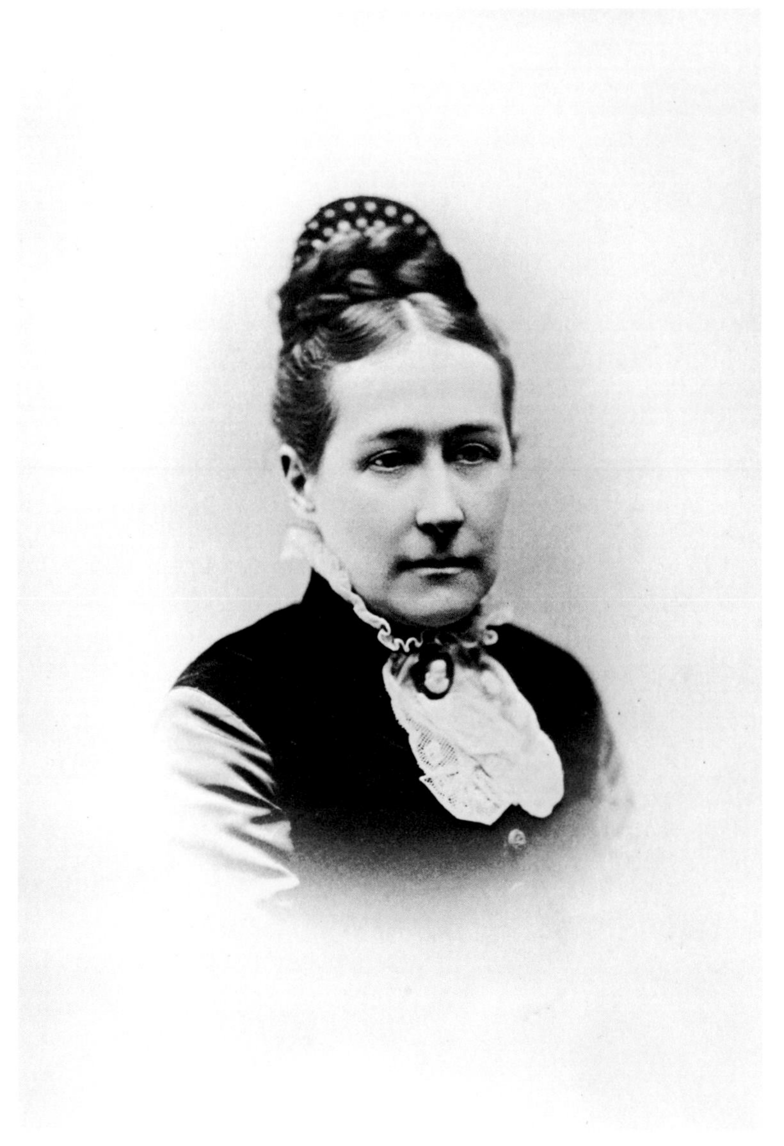

Emma D. Sewall

E*mma Duncan Crooker* was born on September 17, 1836, in Bath, Maine, to Charles Crooker and Rachel Sewall. Charles was one of Bath's early lumber merchants and shipbuilders, and at the height of his career, his company, C & W. D. Crooker, was among the foremost shipbuilders in the world. Emma's mother, Rachel, was a descendant of John Sewall, the first Sewall to come to Maine from Massachusetts in the mid-1600s. The Crookers lived comfortably in a large Greek revival mansion built by Charles and still standing today.

Almost nothing is known of Emma's childhood. Two older siblings died before she was born, but by the time she was five her parents had had two more daughters, Juliette and Adelaide Lydia. In 1852 the girls' mother died of consumption after a long illness and a life devoted to evangelical religion. Interestingly enough, her obituary expounded on her religious tendencies to an unusually elaborate extent for a woman. In fact, Rachel's obituary provided more information than Emma's did sixty years later.

> *In this city, 7th inst., of consumption, Mrs. Rachel Sewall, wife of Charles Crooker, Esq., aged fifty-five. She was a firm believer in the doctrines of evangelical religion—and in her last illness was remarkably sustained by the consolations of the gospel which she had so long professed. And, though the messenger of death came in the midst of great*

usefulness, in the very meridian of life, and with the most flattering of prospects, she was perfectly resigned to her situation—and awaited her final dissolution with a calmness and composure becoming the Christian.

Emma was sixteen at the time of her mother's death and as the oldest child probably inherited a considerable burden of responsibility. It may have been at least partially as a result of her mother's death that she began to turn inward, for she would always be remembered as being shy and introspective.

A year after Rachel's death, Charles Crooker retired from shipbuilding to devote himself to his family and to a growing interest in botany, which he pursued in an outbuilding behind his home. He evidently remained seriously involved in botany for many years, because in this latter part of his life he was commonly referred to as "Dr." Crooker. With Charles at home, Emma saw first hand the pleasures and challenges presented by his scientific explorations. By all accounts Charles was a kind and generous father and almost certainly the primary role model in Emma's life. Educated in Bath schools and active on various school committees, he placed great stock in education and communicated that value to Emma. Charles's love of learning and intellectual ambitions were passed on to his eldest daughter—normally an inheritance reserved for sons then—and may well have filled the void Emma must have felt following her mother's death.

It is my feeling that her father's influence was most likely the source of Emma's appealing contradictions in character. On the one hand she was always known as shy, but underneath her reserved exterior lived a spirited and insistent mind with a drive for knowledge and creative expression. My assumption is that Charles was instrumental in his eldest daughter's character development from the time she was a young girl. It is interesting to note that Emma never embraced a religious doctrine with her whole being, as her mother did.

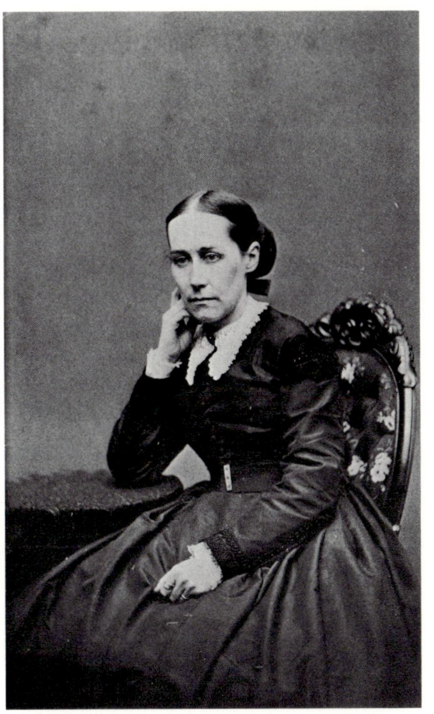

Emma as a young woman.

In 1854, when Emma was eighteen and had completed her education in the Bath schools, Charles sent her to the Ipswich Female Seminary in Ipswich, Massachusetts. Founded in 1826, Ipswich was one of the most prominent secondary schools for women in the country, and Charles's decision to send Emma there reflected his confidence in her intellectual promise. Like most of the school's students, she studied there for two years.

Ipswich insisted on rigid discipline in studies and prayer seven days a week. Students rose at 4:45 A.M. in summer and 5:45 A.M. in winter, with lights out by 9:00 P.M. The curriculum was rigorous and included instruction in history, science, mathematics, astronomy, philosophy, foreign languages, and calisthenics. It was also noted for its fine-art classes, which may have provided Emma with her first serious exposure to painting and drawing.

Emma apparently embraced Ipswich with her whole being and adopted its motto—"Love of study, delight in knowledge"—as her own. The high standards expected of her there were a natural extension of her father's influence, and she emerged from the school a self-motivated scholar, a gift she would always cherish and cultivate. She would continue to study French, history, and literature all her life, to keep up with newspapers and current events throughout the country, and would be remembered by one of her granddaughters as "an unusually talented woman and a great reader, with a vast knowledge of history."

As a young woman, Emma was far from beautiful. She came from a family of notoriously large-boned and heavy-set people, and her features were somewhat masculine. What she lacked in beauty, however, must have been more than compensated for by her strength of character. Portraits taken of her as a young woman reveal a knowingness in her eyes that supercedes her austerity. Perhaps it was Emma's intellect that attracted the young and promising Arthur Sewall a few years after her graduation from Ipswich.

Arthur Sewall and Emma Crooker were third cousins—both descended from the same John Sewall—and presumably knew each

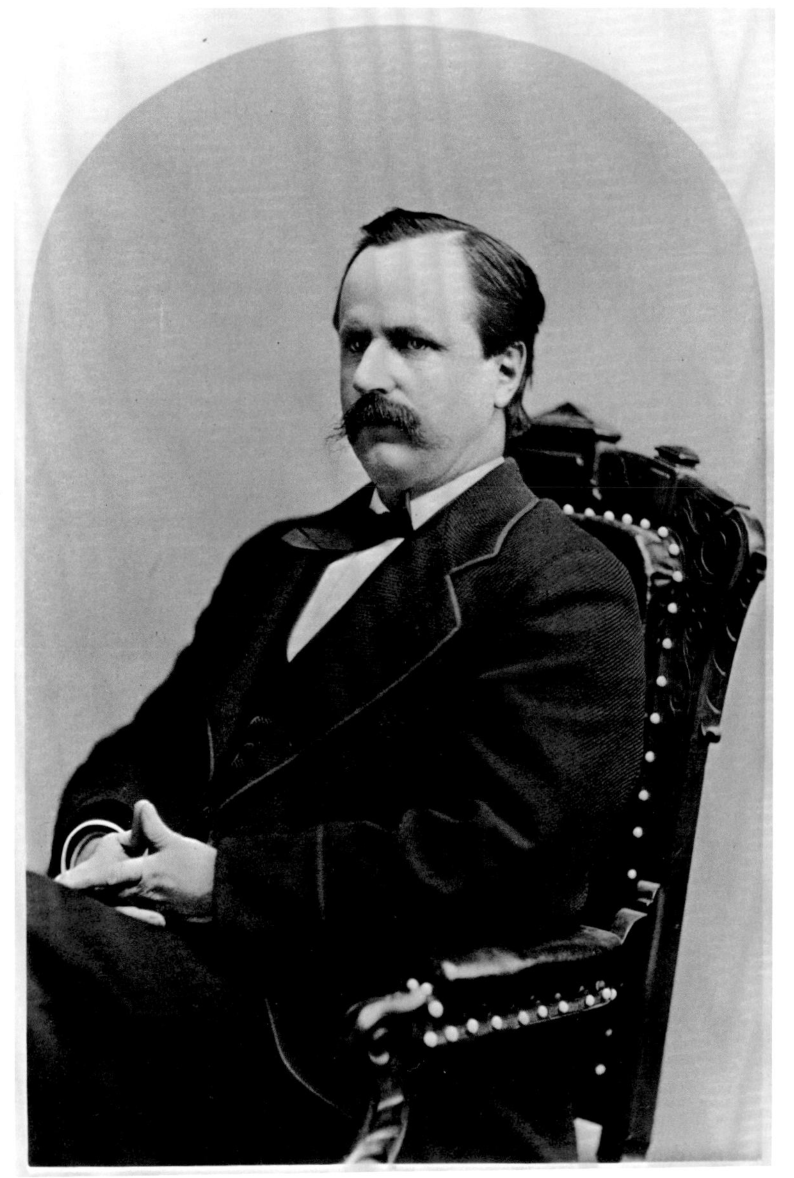

Arthur Sewall

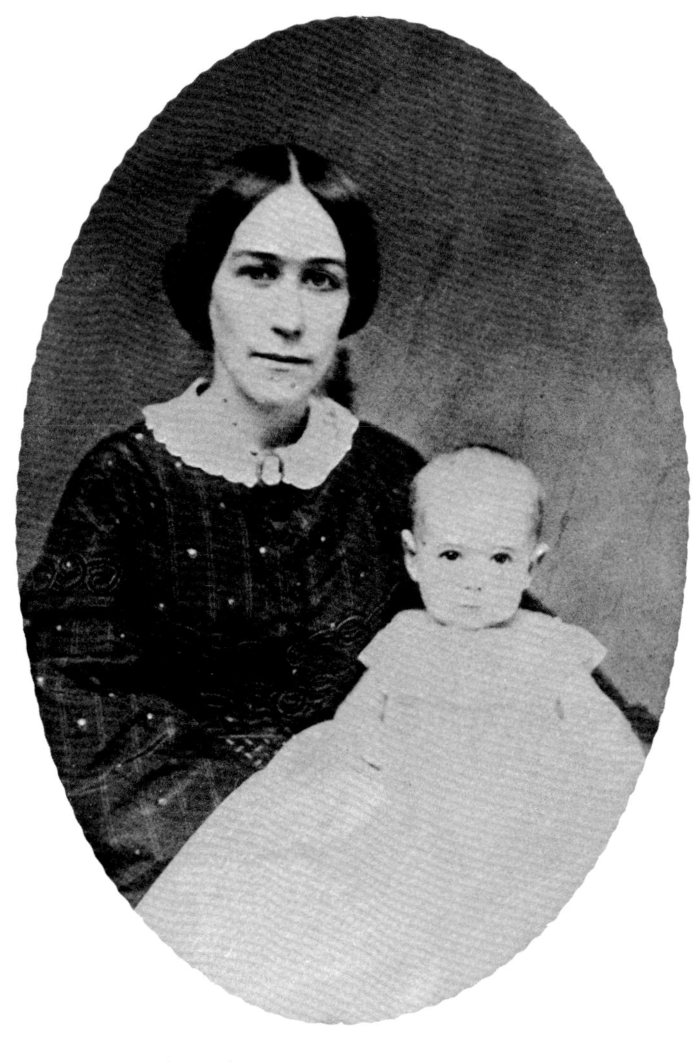

Emma and her son William, about 1862.

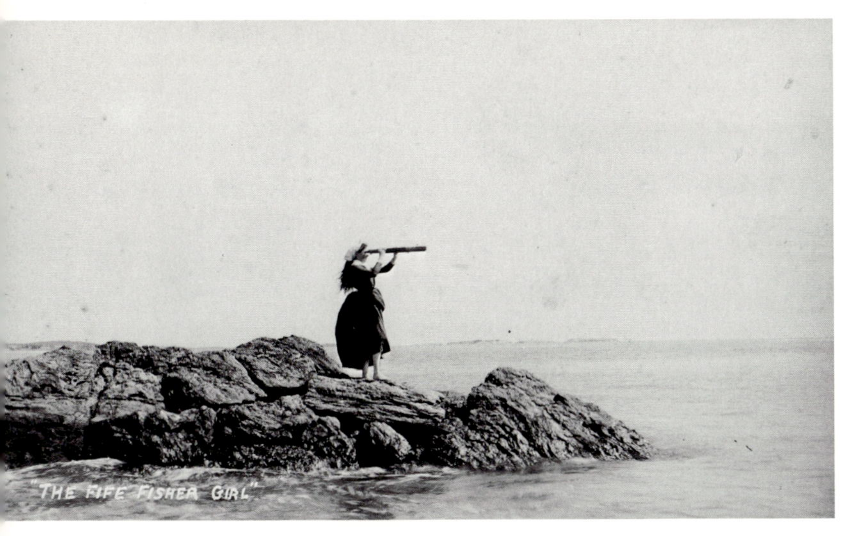

He Cometh Not—Alice Cutler on the rocks at Small Point.

other growing up in Bath. Though probably raised with similar values and expectations as Emma was, Arthur ended his formal education in his teens when he joined his father's shipbuilding business. By the time he married Emma in 1859, when Emma was twenty-three and he was twenty-four, Arthur had already been in the shipbuilding business for himself for five years. During a forty-year career, "The Maritime Prince" would go on to found one of the most successful shipbuilding firms in the world and to build a staggering total of ninety-five sailing ships, including the 3,000-ton *Rappahannock*, the largest wooden ship of its day. He would also become well-known in banking, railroads, and national politics.

Although business required some degree of sociability on his part, Arthur was by nature a reserved, self-contained man. Like Emma, he valued his privacy, his work, and his family. The couple soon had two sons, Harold Marsh Sewall in 1860 and William Dunning Sewall in 1861, and three years later a third son, Dummer, who died when he was two. Their family life apparently was a happy one.

While the Civil War raged in the South, Bath became known as the shipbuilding capital of the world, and Arthur's business flourished. About 1873 the young Sewall family moved into a new Victorian mansion, opulent in its woodwork and filled with fine antiques from around the world. As one visitor described it, "The spacious hall with its heavy walnut carving and moose's antlers, the parlors with their elegant bronzes, choice etchings and paintings and mellow chime-clocks, (Arthur's) private office with its polished andirons, artistic decorations and luxurious upholstering, and the countless beauties and comforts accessible to a man of fortune, combine to make one of the handsomest and most attractive homes in our state." Arthur himself was described as looking "somewhat like a prosperous Turkish pasha" in his blue and gilded smoking jacket.

Shortly after the Sewalls were settled, Arthur's niece from Brookline, Massachusetts, joined them. For the sixteen years she

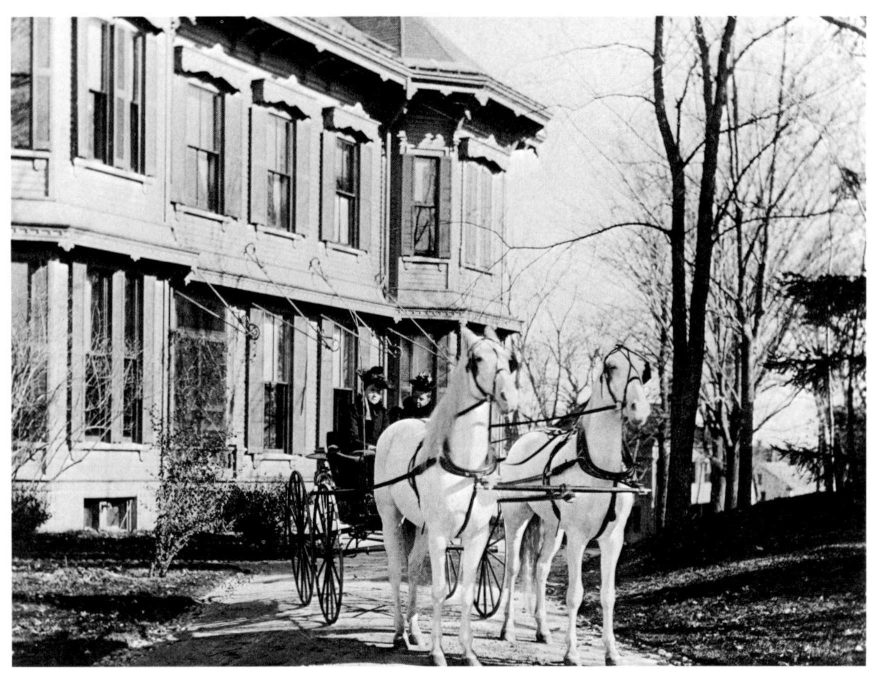

Emma and Alice Cutler in front of the Sewall home.

lived with them, Alice Cutler provided Emma with domestic help and, more importantly, became a close companion and soul mate in the intellectual and artistic realms. Presumably, it's the only such friendship Emma ever had.

Arthur and Emma's home became a perfect reflection of genteel New England society. Emma was "reserved, quite shy with strangers, yet very warm hearted, intellectual, and outgoing in thought." Arthur was known as a "sociable man, devoted to his friends and beloved by them." As a successful businessman and a key figure in the Democratic party, he lived the kind of public life that was probably anathema to his privacy-loving wife. It was not uncommon for the Sewalls to entertain such dignitaries as the governor, congressmen, and even President Harrison. It is not known if Emma was secretly reluctant to fulfill her social obligations as the wife of a prominent businessman—even if she did enjoy a good intellectual discussion; but, the fact that all of my interviews with relatives who remember Emma refer to her shy and reserved nature, and her reclusive tendencies in later years is just cause for speculation. George Little, in *Genealogical and Family History of the State of Maine*, described her character in succinct and contradictory terms by saying, "She was a woman of quiet and refined tastes, who for years made her home a true center of culture and society." How could a woman of "quiet tastes" make her home a "center of culture and society" without internal tension and sacrifice? One might conclude that there were times when the Sewalls' social life infringed on Emma's need for study and introspection.

Despite their widely diverging interests, Emma and Arthur's devotion to one another was absolute. Just as Emma supported Arthur in business and politics, he supported and encouraged her in her artistic and intellectual endeavors. Whether he understood her or not, he apparently accepted the fact that her needs transcended those of being a wife and mother and that she would always hold part of herself in reserve. She often took trips away from Bath or, at home, simply retired to her room for lengthy periods.

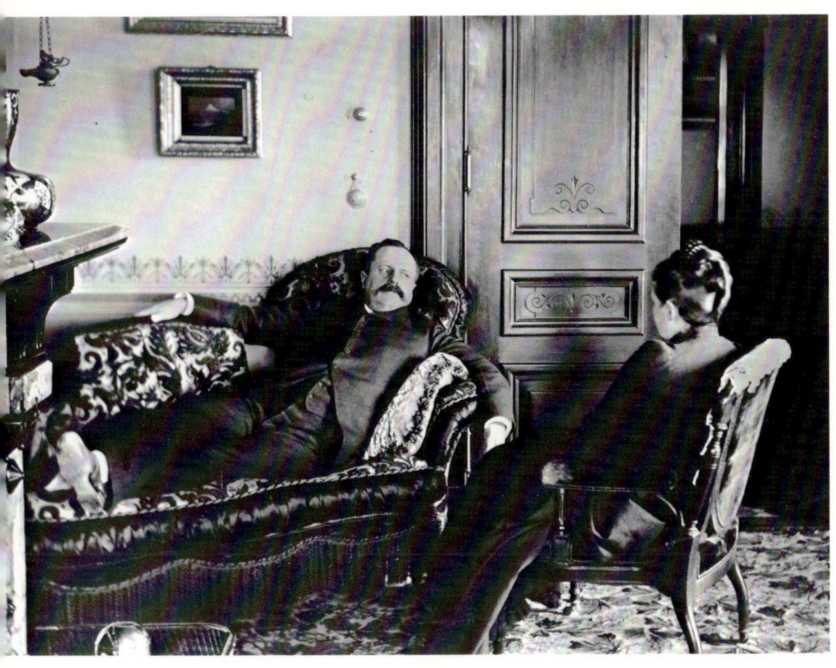

Emma and Arthur at home.

While their sons were growing up, Emma often went to the White Mountains in western Maine for the summer, where she had visited as a child. Taking the boys and probably Alice Cutler with her, she begged off from the "company season" in Bath, when traffic through the Sewalls' home could be particularly heavy. While little Harrie and Willie fished and trapped, Emma went for walks and horseback rides and spent cherished hours alone in her room.

Emma wrote home to Arthur (whose business usually kept him in Bath) almost daily, and her letters reveal warmth and intimacy between them, as well as a mutual respect for their differences. Most of her letters consisted of pleasant minutiae of family life, comments about her health, and endearments to Arthur. It is clear that she missed him terribly but needed a rest and change from Bath. Her privacy was such a valued commodity that in one letter she made a reference to hiding in her room to avoid visits from other holiday seekers who knew her. Her letter stated, "I saw Mrs.—coming down the road, so I went off upstairs." She wrote to Arthur of her deep appreciation and enjoyment of the countryside, the freedom and expanse of space, and the beauty of the landscape. The pleasure she felt in being there ignited her creative urges, and these were further inspired by her brother-in-law, Joseph Ropes, of Salem, Massachusetts, who painted landscapes. Emma often mentioned watching him in her letters home.

In an undated letter written from Mount Blue one summer, Emma described watching her brother-in-law paint. "Mr. Ropes has been out this morning and painted a lovely little view—out back of the house. Just a view of the mountains and a bit of the field—and bushes and golden rod—almost nothing but yet a bit of summer. I watched him while he made it and it grew like magic under his fingers. I have never enjoyed a little picture so much." This may have been Emma's first awareness of a desire to express herself visually. She also wrote, "I have learned to *see* landscapes . . ." It was a talent she would employ not long after, when she began to take her first photographs.

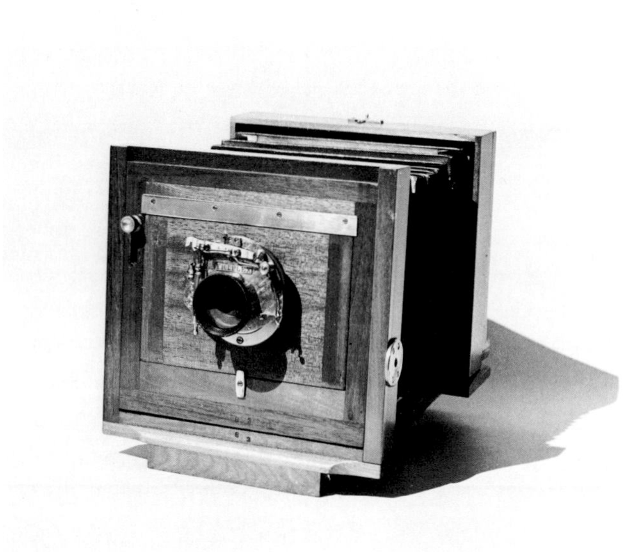

One of Emma's two cameras, thought to be made by the American Optical Company.

By 1884 Harold and William Sewall had graduated from college. Emma, now forty-eight, seized upon her freedom and spent from March to December that year riding the rails, sometimes with Arthur or her sons, sometimes alone. Her shy nature did not prevent her from traveling well beyond New England, for a large scrapbook she kept contains ticket stubs from Buffalo, Albany, Chicago, San Francisco, and Portland, Oregon. Emma must have relished the quietude she found on these trips. The ever-changing landscapes must have been a feast for her eyes, easily inspiring her tendency toward the picturesque. Traveling far from home may also have given her a new aesthetic acuity toward her own visual landscape at home in Bath.

It was at one of these stops on her 1884 trip that Emma purchased her first camera and, inspired perhaps by the dramatic landscapes she saw from her train window, began taking photographs. The glass plates that survive from that trip—random snapshots of Western landscapes and prairie towns—are clearly those of a novice. But Emma continued to take pictures after her return to Maine, and by the late 1880s she was obviously at ease with her heavy 5 x 7″ wooden field camera and the cumbersome glass plates and wooden holders. She had a strong command of lighting and composition and had refined her darkroom technique. Like her father, who began a second career in botany when he was fifty-six, Emma was in her fifties when she made photography the passion of her life.

Born only eleven years after the French scientist Joseph Niépce produced the first photographic image, Emma had the good fortune to take up photography at a time when the medium was changing rapidly. Prior to the 1880s, photographic technique required immediate development of the glass plates—the wet-plate method—and thus prevented photographers from straying very far from their studios. Consequently, photography was practiced mainly by journeymen who had little time or need for the aesthetics of the craft. A different environment was needed to produce photographs that were artistic in nature, rather than a novelty, and this came about in the

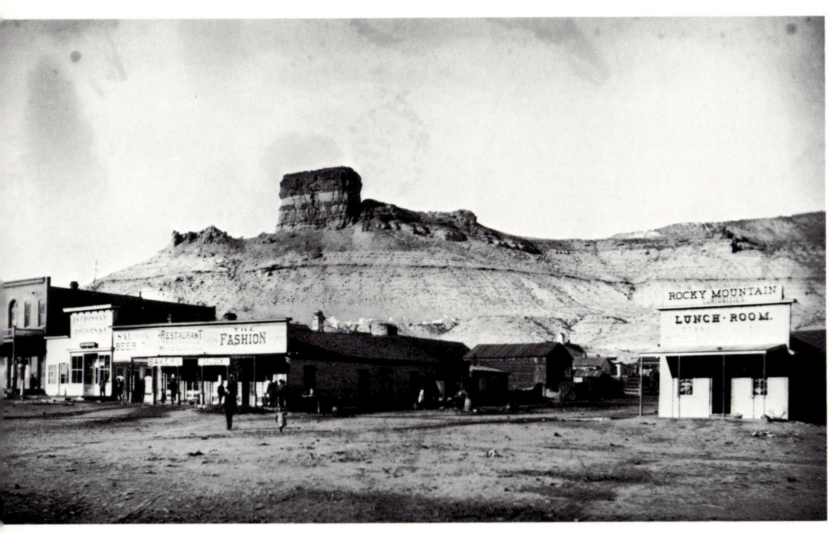

Gun River City—UPRR (Union Pacific Railroad)—
One of Emma's early photographs, taken during train trip of 1884.

1880s with the introduction of the dry-plate method. Photographers could now develop plates at their leisure and could stray as far from their studios as they wished. The dry-plate method of development revolutionized photography and resulted in a rapid increase in the commercial production of photographic materials and equipment and a simplification of the photographic process. It also brought instant popularity to photography and resulted in its birth as an art form.

Along with photography's new popularity came the emergence of photography clubs. Amateur photographers—people devoted to art photography rather than to commercial studio work—joined together all over western Europe and the U.S. to hold exhibits, critique each other's work, and keep up with the latest techniques. These groups launched photography's first art movement, called Pictorialism, which flourished from the late 1880s to 1923. Pictorial photography was initially influenced by the Impressionist movement in painting, which resulted in diffused and romanticized images of nature, and later by realism and the "personal eye," exemplified by detailed studies in composition and viewpoint. Emma's work was a blend of both the romantic and realistic aspects of Pictorialism.

Maine provided Emma with a rich vein of material for her photographs. All her adult life she had studied local history, traced the genealogies of many local families, and collected Indian lore and tales of shipbuilders and sailors. Now, camera in hand, she set out to do something similar with photography. Taking pictures of country people working the land and sea, she recorded a way of life that was vanishing before the quickening pace of the Industrial Age. I believe Emma was well aware that she was documenting a disappearing life-style, a life-style with a certain quality of innocence never to be found again.

She took her strongest photographs of country people performing everyday tasks—a farmer collecting eggs in his hat, clam diggers in starched shirts and suspenders, children collecting firewood on the beach. She caught these people in the act of living and portrayed

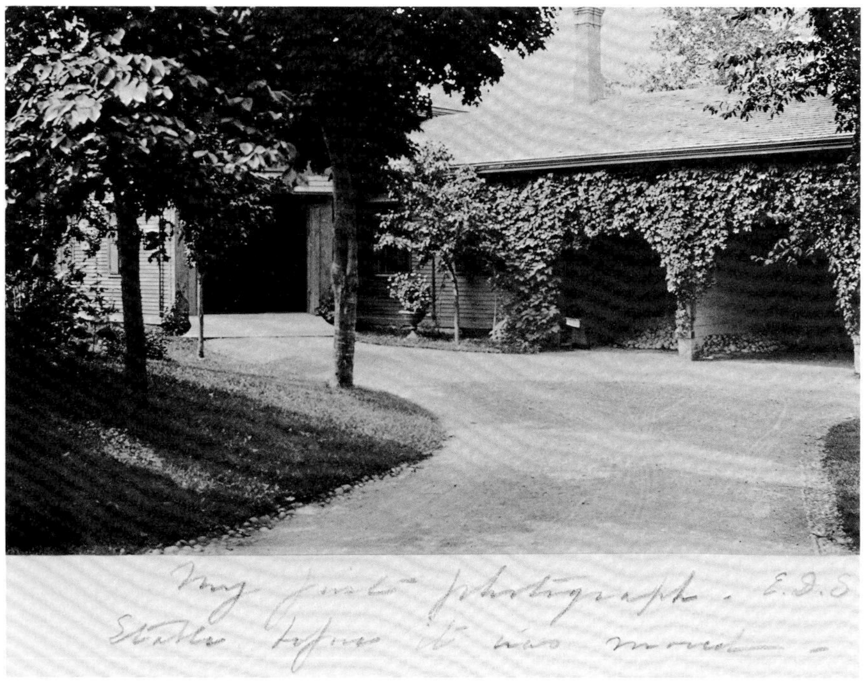

My first photograph—E. D. S. Stable before it was moved.—
Emma's statement that she has arrived at a photographic consciousness.

them as if they were royalty, ennobling them with a beautifully soft and subtle light that reflected an almost spiritual reverence for them. She had great respect for these people as well as a deep curiosity and fascination.

Emma's choice of subject matter was personal. "The process of choosing what to photograph is as complex and multi-faceted as the photographer himself," writes photographer Berenice Abbott, "for art is primarily autobiographical." The beauty Emma saw in her subjects came from a longing for a life-style she could only glimpse and never be part of. As a woman of privileged upbringing and great wealth, Emma was set apart from her subjects. She romanticized working people like other Pictorialists of her era, but for Emma the reasons were intrinsic rather than stylistic: she admired and perhaps envied a simpler, more direct relationship with nature and the world. Her own life, by contrast, was overly complex—full of social and dress constraints, protocol, and demands that had little to do with what really mattered in life. The few portraits that remain of Emma all show a woman who looks stiff and constrained by the formality of her attire and environment.

Photographing the simplicities of rural life became Emma's way of stripping away all the trappings of her genteel class and of establishing a connection to a universality among men and women—a theme that interested her all her life. For the artist-photographer, the act of photographing transcends class distinctions, but ironically, in Emma's case her best subject matter also reinforced the obvious contrast between her life and theirs. Was she perhaps caught in the middle, not quite comfortable anywhere? In her effort to transcend class through photography, did she perhaps develop a jaded view of her own class? I believe that there did exist the attendant challenge of personal confrontation along with the pleasure and inspiration found in the medium. Nonetheless, the deep respect Emma had for her subject matter enabled her to photograph from the heart. She brought intellect and emotion to her work, and this is one of its great strengths.

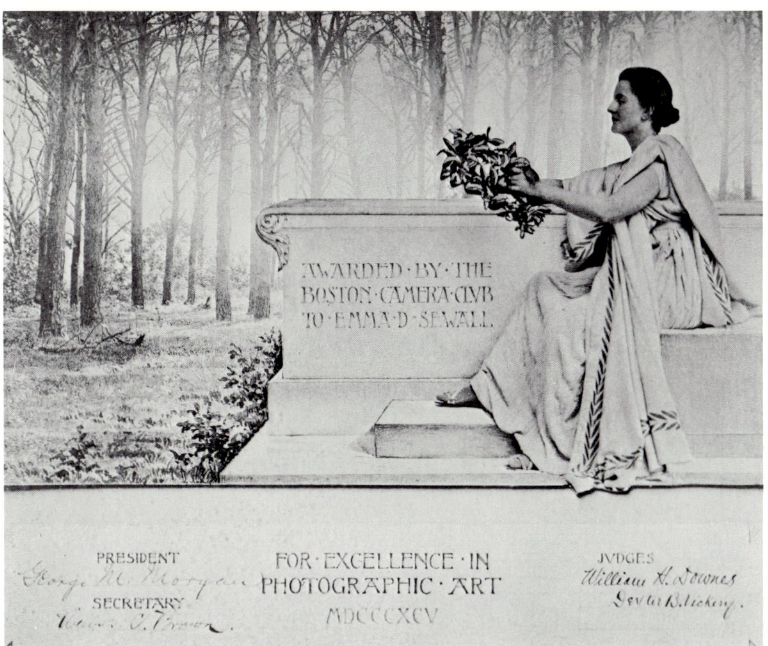

One of Emma's many awards.

By the late 1880s Emma had joined the Postal Photographic Club of Fitchburg, Massachusetts, a well-known group of photo enthusiasts who each month contributed prints for a photo album that, together with a notebook for criticisms, was circulated among the members. Emma's platinum prints began winning prizes in photographic club exhibits, and she soon became one of the club's most prominent members. In April, 1894, when she was invited to join the prestigious Boston Camera Club, she was one of the earliest women to be admitted and, at age fifty-eight, one of the oldest members.

From 1894 to 1898 Emma exhibited annually in Boston and won top awards each year. In 1895, perhaps her most successful year, she received the Boston Camera Club's highest award, the diploma for greatest general excellence for "a group of beautiful compositions, including landscapes, old-fashioned New England interiors, sea views, and genre subjects indoors and in the open air," according to a contemporary Boston newspaper account. "Mrs. Arthur Sewall . . . is one of the foremost women amateurs in the country," the review continued. "Her works all evidence maturity of style; and her technique is equal to the best." Emma's photographs received a similarly enthusiastic reception when she exhibited at the Photo-Club of Paris that same month, where she won a bronze plaque for her entries. In this much-publicized international exhibition, Emma's work hung next to that of such well-known photographers as Alfred Stieglitz and the French photographer Robert Demachy. I find it interesting that Emma chose to take advantage of the Boston club's affiliation with the Photo-Club of Paris rather than pursue exhibitions in other American clubs. Paris must have appealed to Emma's love of history, the French language in which she was proficient, and travel.

Whether or not Emma ever studied with a professional photographer is unknown; she probably didn't, because photography was such a new medium then that there were virtually no schools for it. More likely she relied on books and periodicals such as *American*

Amateur Photographer, a leading journal whose editors included Alfred Stieglitz and in which Emma's work was critiqued in 1895. Nor is much known about Emma's rapport with other photographers. She visited Boston regularly (where she stayed with Alice Cutler's family), and she attended the opening of at least one of her Paris exhibitions, probably in 1895, because the exhibition catalog from that year was among her remaining belongings. But given her shyness and the fact that she was much older than most of her photographic contemporaries, she probably had little to do with the social aspects of photo clubs and exhibitions.

Like other amateur photographers, Emma made her own prints. It was part of the artistic process. The preferred method in her day was the platinum process. She bought platinum-coated paper, exposed her plates in daylight, contact printed them onto the platinum paper, and then went through a three-chemical process to develop and fix them. Finally, she washed the prints for about forty-five minutes. Platinum prints are characterized by their wide tonal range, with rich blacks and neutral, silver-gray midtones. The process was largely abandoned after World War I when the cost of platinum rose dramatically.

In April of 1896, a group of Emma's photographs again won first prize for the most artistic merit at the annual exhibition of the Boston Camera Club. Her work was described with high praise in New England newspapers. The following excerpt is from the *Bath Independent*. "A Bath lady, Mrs. Emma D. Sewall, won the diploma for the exhibition of photographs having the most artistic merit at the annual exhibition held under the auspices of the Boston Camera Club last week. The *Boston Transcript* said, 'Mrs. Sewall's framed group of landscapes and figures is fully as interesting as was that of last year. The jury commended especially the *Harvest Time*, which shows the interior of a New England barn, with apples, pumpkins, grain, hay, farming tools, etc., in picturesque confusion; a ploughing scene entitled *Indian Summer,* which is certainly notable for it's exquisite atmosphere; and *Autumn Ploughing*, another bucolic, with an

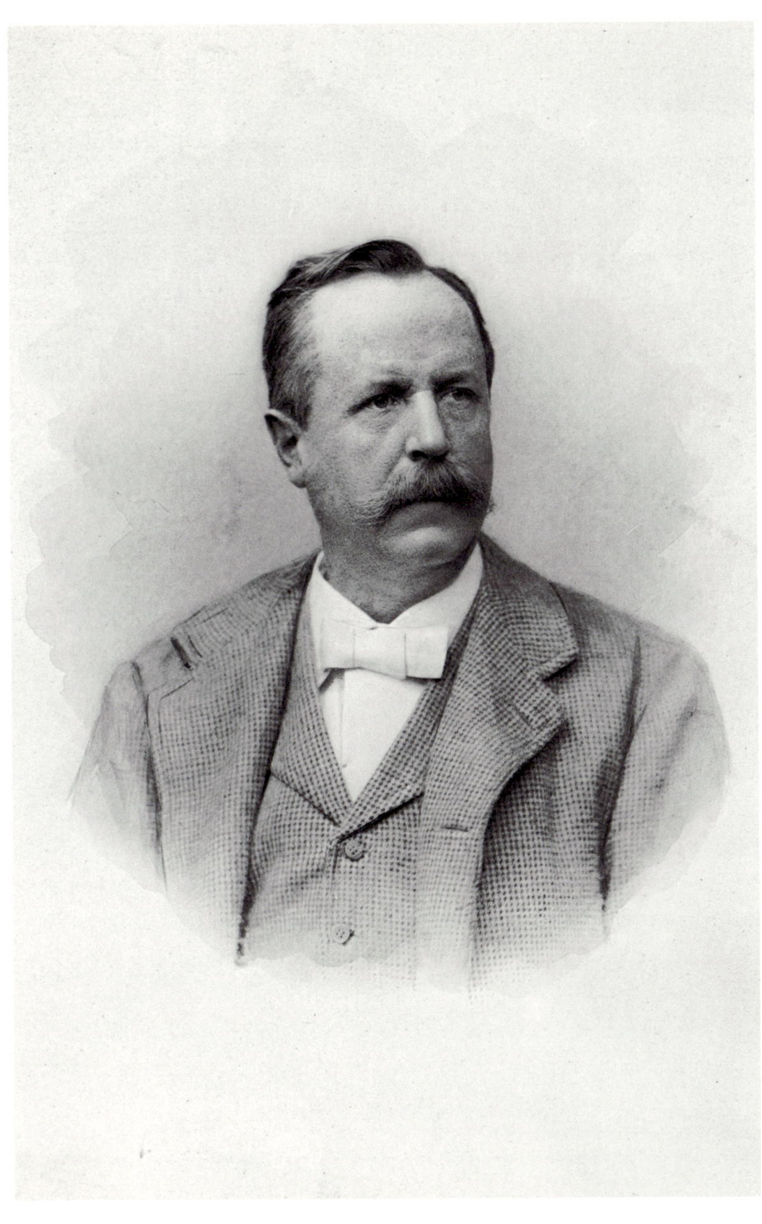

Vice presidential campaign portrait of Arthur Sewall, 1896.

immense tree stem in the foreground, a pair of horses and a man, and a pretty distance with farmhouses and barns. We find also of more than equal interest her *Study for Miss Wilkins*, which is full of character and humor; and *The Village Blacksmith*, which is remarkable for the success with which difficulties only too familiar to all amateur photographers have been overcome.'"

Emma was at her peak as a photographer, but beginning in July it was suddenly Arthur's name that was in the newspapers, and not always in the glowing terms accorded his wife. A lifelong Democrat well known for his devotion to his country, Arthur had served as a delegate to his party's presidential conventions in 1872, 1880, and 1884, and as a member of the Democratic National Committee in 1888 and 1892. His party affiliation made him an anomaly in a strongly Republican state, where he had never held an elective office higher than that of city alderman. To make matters worse, his own sons were Republicans, a fact the press made use of by asking how Sewall could expect to carry the state if he couldn't even carry his family? Nonetheless, at the 1896 Democratic Convention in July, sixty-year-old Arthur Sewall was nominated on the fifth ballot as the running mate of Presidential candidate William Jennings Bryan. The party's first choice—a man far wealthier than Sewall—had declined to run, in effect making Sewall a compromise candidate. Sewall's appeal was that he was from the East, balancing the fact that Bryan was from the West, and as a man of wealth could contribute bountifully to the campaign. Out of an intense sense of duty and loyalty to his country, Arthur accepted, despite the disruptions it would mean to his family life.

The campaign against the Republican ticket of William McKinley and Garrett A. Hobart was a fierce one, perhaps nowhere more so than in Bath. The initial pride Bath took in its native son—whose shipbuilding industry employed hundreds of local men and had brought international acclaim to the city—soon turned to sniping. Newspaper reporting in the 1890s, says author Mark Hennessey in his book *Sewall Ships of Steel*, was radically partisan. "There was no

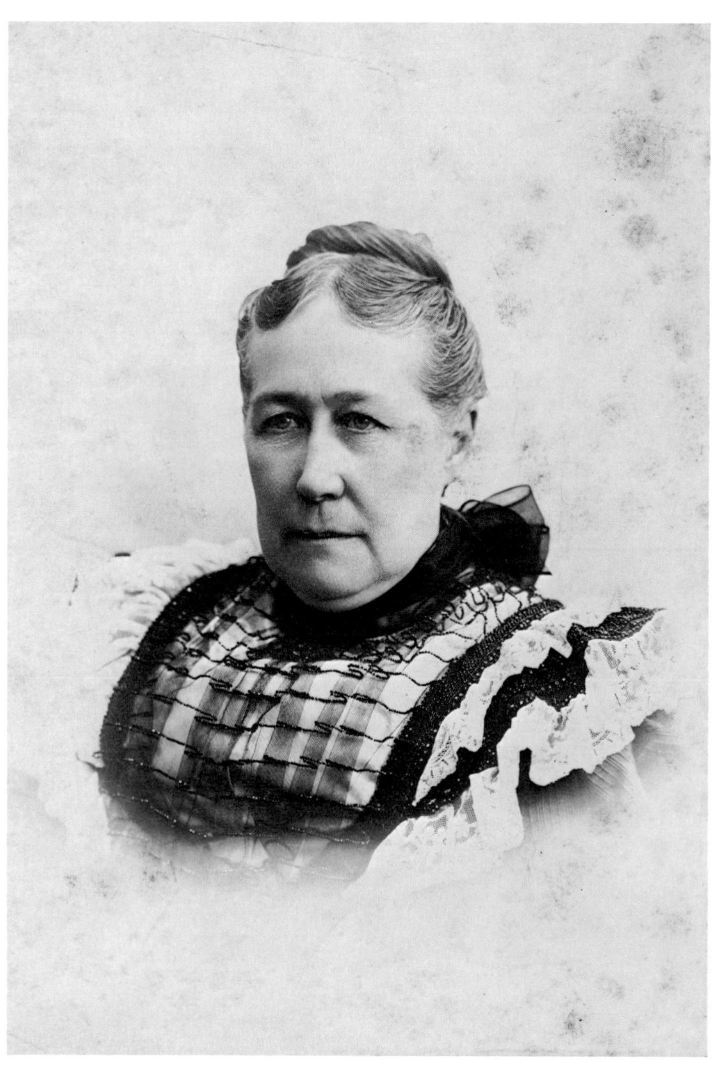

Portrait of Emma taken during the 1896 campaign.

such thing as political issue with two sides, and the opposition's candidates were, to all intents and purposes, scoundrels, or relations thereof. The popular school of thought held that it was the duty of a newspaper, immediately political battle lines were formed, to open fire with main and secondary batteries and continue the battle until not an enemy principle was standing. If innocent reputations fell along with principles under this barrage, it was too bad. Politics in the Nineties had considerable in common with modern warfare." Bath's three newspapers, all Republican, ran a stream of articles viciously attacking Sewall.

The intensity of the criticism came as a shock to both the Sewalls. Emma was hounded by the press for pictures of herself and information on her life. Much was made of her age and reclusivity. Who was she? Would she be suited to public life as the wife of the vice-president? Time and time again she refused to meet with the press or sit for a portrait, but finally, in hopes of being left alone, she relented and sat for her portrait at a local photography studio. Not surprisingly, the volume of her own photographic work fell off that year.

When the Bryan-Sewall ticket went down to defeat in the general election (though only by a four-percent edge in the popular vote), Arthur finally dropped out of politics, much to Emma's relief. The hostile nature of the campaign seemed to be a turning point in Emma's life, reinforcing her natural inclination to withdraw. Worn down emotionally as well as physically, she and Arthur both turned their attention now to the construction of a large summer home, The Dunes, at Small Point, a coastal community at the mouth of the Kennebec River.

Often accompanied by Arthur, Emma began to photograph again. In 1897 she won the "Best Figure Composition" award at the Boston Camera Club for *The Search* and *The Village Blacksmith*. In 1898 the Boston Camera Club also awarded her an engraved silver bowl for *When the Day's Work is Done*, her image of a woman reading her Bible by the dim light of a single candle. This photograph was

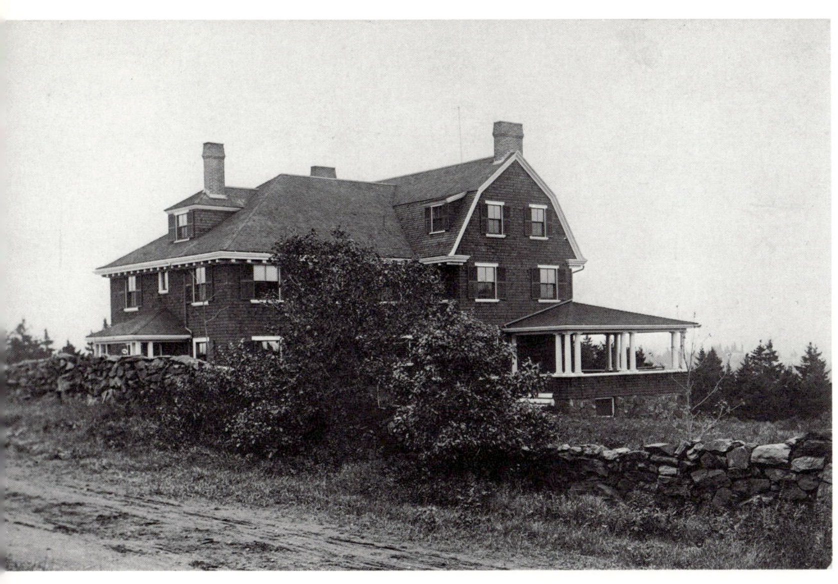

Emma's sanctuary, The Dunes, Small Point, Maine.

also entered in the 1898 Photo-Club of Paris exhibit, where Emma received a silver-plated medal of honor.

Whether consciously or not, Emma's title of *When the Day's Work is Done* foreshadowed the end of her days as an exhibitor. In the years that followed, several of Emma's Small Point photographs appeared on the pages of Bath newspapers, but she never exhibited again.

With the completion of The Dunes—described in one newspaper as "the finest summer residence on the Maine coast west of Bar Harbor"—in June of 1899, Emma finally had a sanctuary in the place she loved best. She could never be like the people in her photographs, but now she could attempt to manifest a life-style more akin to her spiritual and artistic inclinations. Ironically, one of the first photographic projects she undertook there, in the summers of 1899 and 1900, was a comprehensive study of the interior of The Dunes. Perhaps she wanted no more than to leave proof of the way she lived for future generations, thus fulfilling her self-appointed role as a historian. But juxtaposed with her photographs of Small Point natives and landscapes, the formal elegance in the cottage photographs makes a lasting impression of Emma as a divided soul. Emma loved The Dunes, but she was constantly aware of the distorting influence of wealth. One of the entries in her scrapbook is a newspaper column entitled "Just Folks" that contains a poem that obviously struck a chord in her own thinking. These are the last two stanzas:

> Envy no man's costlier dress,
> It may cover keen distress;
> In the rich man's home may be
> Loneliness and misery;
> And the great man, brave and good,
> If we only understood,
> May be suffering bitter woes
> Than his humbler brother knows.

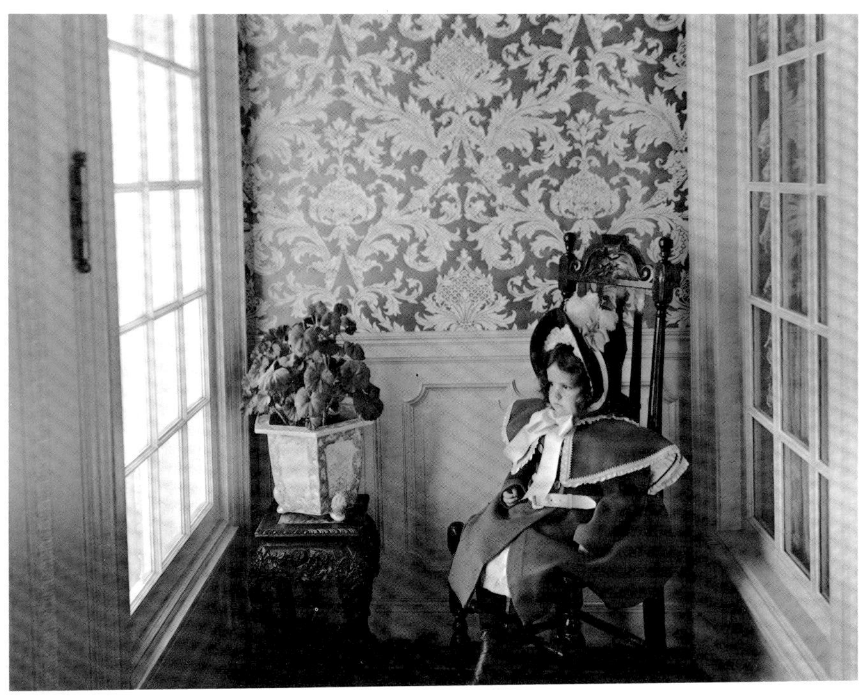

Emma's granddaughter Dorothy posing in the front entry hall of her father's house c. 1899 in Bath, Maine.

Each must feel the hurt of pain,
Each must take his share of rain;
None can go through life without
Coming face to face with doubt,
And the price of fame and gold
May be bitter griefs untold;
Troubles come to every man
Though he lives the best he can.

The happiness that came to Emma with Arthur's retirement and the completion of The Dunes was short-lived. In 1899 her niece and favored companion, Alice Cutler, who earlier had lived with the Sewalls for sixteen years, died. An anonymous tribute to her—more than likely written by Emma—in the *Bath Daily Times* said, "So glad was her service to all who needed her, one saw that her special capability in adapting herself to circumstances, arose from her wish to lighten the burdens and sweeten the lives that touched hers. . . We shall recall her always as glad and free beyond the most of us and have no difficulty in perceiving her a spiritual being. . ." The next year, having enjoyed only two summer seasons at The Dunes, Arthur died. He had been ill for some time with Bright's Disease, an incurable kidney disease. Emma was sixty-four years old and devasted by the losses.

Emma lived nineteen more years, but her career as a photographer was over. She resigned from the Boston Camera Club shortly after Arthur's death and rarely photographed again. In 1901 she gave her camera to her grandson with the following note: "I give this with my dearest love to my grandson Arthur Sewall, because he knows better than any of the other children how much I have enjoyed my camera. I hope he will take good care of it and leave it to someone who will value it."

Her mourning for those closest to her, and her own advancing age, took on an added sense of loss with the knowledge that her photography career was over—and over much too soon. Relatives

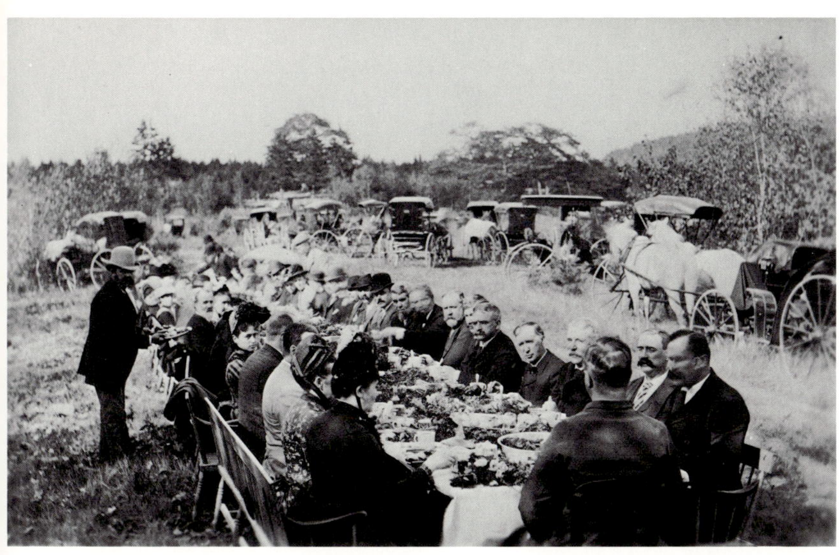

Picnic at Foster's Point given in honor of Arthur Sewall, August 14, 1889. Arthur is seated at the head of the table, with Emma on his left.

old enough to remember Emma recall a recluse who kept to her room for days at a time. In all but the coldest months of the year she lived at The Dunes, sustained by the proximity of the sea, the sound of the waves, and the smell of the fresh salt air entering every room of her home—the very home where I would discover her photographs years later.

Within this solitude Emma began the final era of her life. Although she would feel overwhelmed by loneliness and isolation at times, her thirst for knowledge and artistic expression never waned. From photography she turned to scholarship and writing. Perhaps it was also during this time that she completed the two large and impressive scrapbooks that make up the primary sources of information on her adult life. One scrapbook, eighteen by twenty-four inches, and leather bound, is labelled *The Great Political Campaign of '96 Volume I.* It is more than two inches thick and contains a comprehensive documentation of the Bryan-Sewall campaign from newspapers all over the United States and France. She did not censor the bad press, but included what appears to be everything that was published.

The other scrapbook is distinctly autobiographical, starting in 1883 with railroad ticket stubs documenting Arthur and Emma's many transcontinental journeys. She included clippings of Arthur's numerous professional affiliations; articles on history, genealogy (with her corrections noted in the margins), and the Sewall family; poetry; and mementos of her photographic career and awards. The clippings were from newspapers from around the country and often included articles on obscure exotica: "Lost Race Lived On Lonely Isle—Huge Monuments Left by Ancient People of Easter Island, 2000 miles from Mainland." An article describing a picnic given in honor of Arthur on August 14, 1889 was quite entertaining : "Our Arthur—Bath Citizens Recognize a Man of Public Spirit and Value—At Last!—Regardless of Party They Entertain Pres. Sewall at Foster's Point." The menu consisted of "20 bushels of clams, 100 lobsters, 2 barrels of sweet corn, 225 lbs. of chicken, 1 bushel of onions, 20

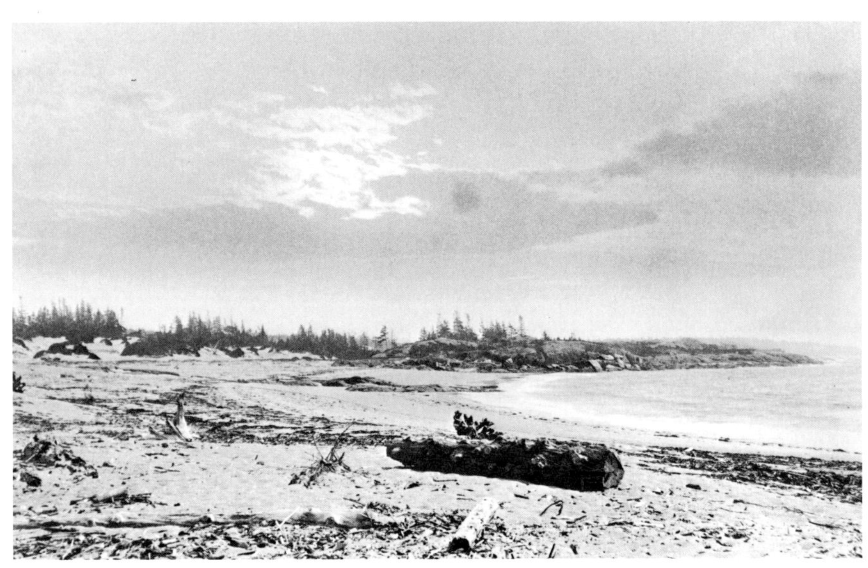

A Lonely Shore from *The Rivers and Marshes of Small Point.*

dozen eggs, 20 lbs. of coffee, ½ barrel of pickels, 25 quarts cream, and 30 lbs. of butter." The scrapbook ends about the time of Emma's death with an article entitled, "The Absolute Loneliness And Isolation Of The Individual Soul"

> *You who read this—man or woman, old or young—must be conscious very often of a feeling of isolation.*
>
> *Each human soul is as much a separate organism as any one of the great planets or suns. And it is eternal and immortal, and capable of infinite development.*
>
> *Each of us must do his work alone, conquer himself alone, fight out his fights alone.*
>
> *At birth we come into the world alone, not understanding and not understood by others.*
>
> *At death we go out alone and come back alone to the mysterious source whence we came.*
>
> *We have our friendships, our affections, our interests in each other. But our real lives, of work, we must live by ourselves.*

For years Emma had collected the folklore and researched the genealogy of Small Point families, and it was during this time that she compiled it into a beautifully lyrical little book called *The Rivers and Marshes of Small Point*, which was published posthumously by her daughter-in-law Mary Sumner Sewall. Emma also composed a one year calendar of daily maxims—some created by her, some quoted from favorite writers and poets of the day—as a Christmas present for her son William in 1905. Read as a whole, these references to knowledge, Puritan ethics, love, time and eternity, and frequently to sorrow and isolation offer an intimate view of Emma's personal thoughts on life and are the closest example of a journal that remains.

Among family members there has always been an air of mystery surrounding Emma, for when I started asking questions about her, no one knew *why* she became so reclusive or *what* she did, alone in her room for days at a time. In addition to working on the projects already mentioned, she spent much of her time alone writing letters of inquiry to other Sewalls throughout New England in her quest to unravel the family genealogy. She had an ongoing correspondence with Joseph Sewall of York, Maine, where many of the earlier Sewalls had settled. She managed to procure a letter dating back to 1700 from Jothan Sewall to Henry Sewall of Bath and an article tracing the Sewall origins in England that dated back to 1066. She collected a variety of antiquated deeds, funeral papers, and sermons from the 1700s. She even had floor plans from a church in York, Maine, and stamps from all over the world.

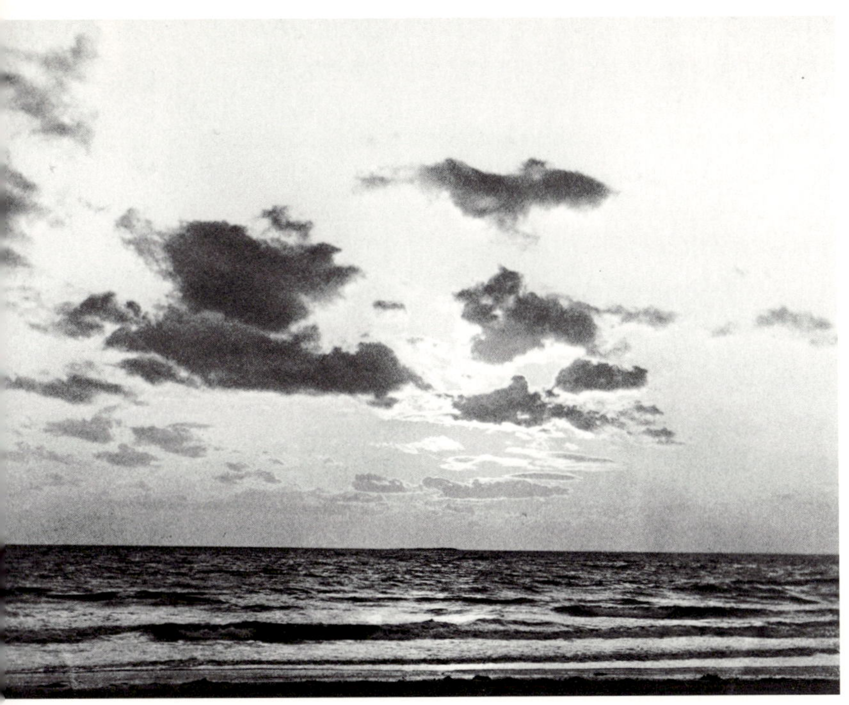

Untitled from *The Rivers and Marshes of Small Point.*

Looking through the books she read, I came across a newspaper clipping that fell out of *The Roadmender*, a book by Michael Fairless (Marjorie Fairless Barber): "Michael Fairless was a woman of much personal grace and distinction, of high intellectual attainment, and great artistic power and culture. Her 'poverty' was voluntarily embraced, and what specially characterized her for those who knew her was her Franciscan love for mankind, for all things, great or small."

There is no doubt that Emma revered a woman like Michael Fairless, and in my mind Emma was a similar kind of woman. From one of her poetry books titled *Prose Pastorals*, I read: "He who knows what sweets and virtues are in the ground, the waters, the plants, the heavens, and how to come at these enchantments, is the rich and royal man." The kind of wealth Emma aspired to was the spiritual wealth that comes from an understanding of man's universality.

On Monday, September 29, 1919, Emma Sewall died at The Dunes. Her brief obituary stated, "She was stricken Sunday and never regained consciousness." There was no information about her or her work; only that she was the daughter, wife, and mother of prominent men. The significance of her life had already begun to fade from view.

Emma's life was that of a pioneering woman determined not to be limited by Puritan tradition and class conformity. In a social climate that generally did not encourage women to express them-

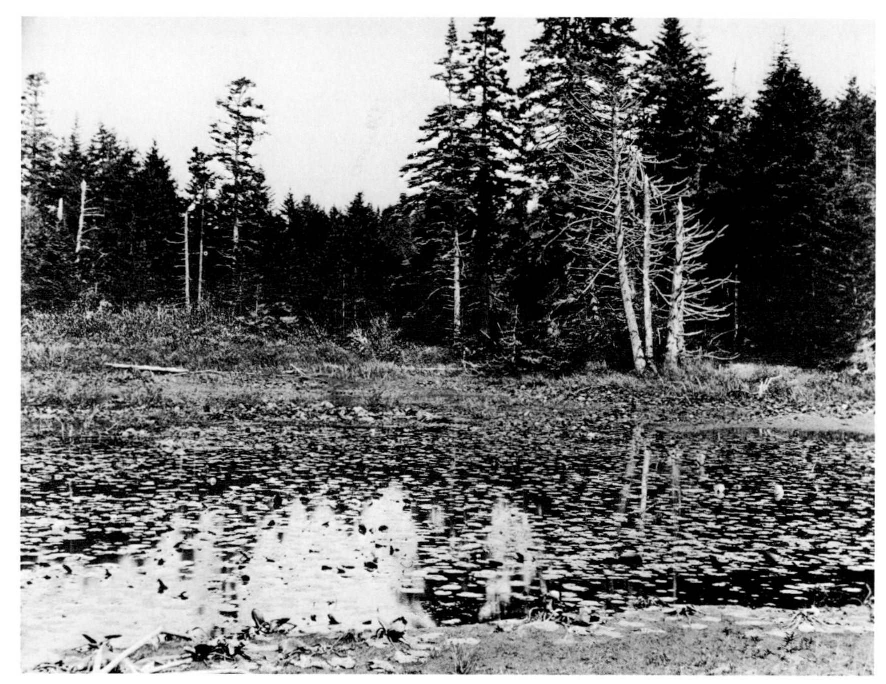

Untitled

selves intellectually or artistically, Emma celebrated her own particular vision and spirit. She was surprisingly prolific for a woman of her age and social standing, and she achieved a remarkable clarity and eloquence of style in a very short time. Her photographic career was short but went swiftly to the top.

Emma clearly loved photography for itself: for the freedom it gave her and the challenge it presented. She must have or she would never have persisted with the hard work and drudgery it involved—the heavy field camera, the glass plates and their bulky wooden holders, the tripod, and the long, tiring hours in the darkroom. The word "pioneer" can also be applied to this strong-willed photographer on a purely physical level. Just imagine her lugging her cumbersome equipment through the rough and rutted woods around Moosehead Lake or through the sand and salt marshes of Small Point. It would take an adventuring kind of individual with an unusually strong artistic drive to bother battling the bugs and heat of summer, the cold winter, and the labor and isolation of it all year-round. But perhaps Emma also felt that photography helped make up for her inability to comply with all the social graces expected of her. She was a woman caught in conflict between propriety and a need for spiritual and creative growth. In a letter to Arthur from the White Mountains one summer, she expressed a desire to make Arthur proud of her artistically. Referring to the artistic influence of Mr. Ropes, she said, ". . . if I could paint, you'd be proud of my pictures some day." Wanting to please the husband she loved so dearly, without compromising her need for artistic and intellectual exploration, was something Emma probably struggled with all her married life. That she succeeded in doing both is a testament to her talent and strength of character.

Despite the fact that she was once lauded as one of the leading female photographers of her day, Emma and her work quickly slipped from view. Her work has never before appeared in a book of American photography. Partly this is an artifact of Emma's time. Photography was a brand new medium and photographers were

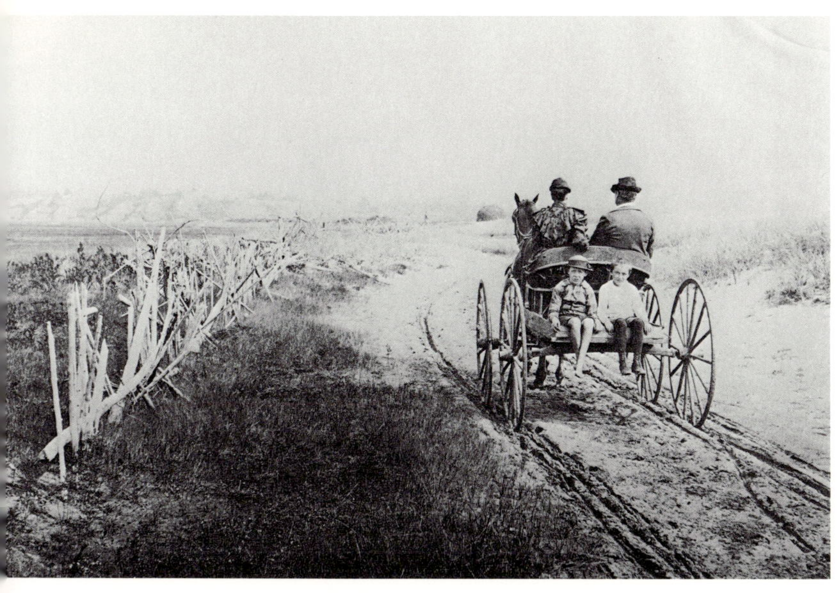

A Morning Drive from *The Rivers and Marshes of Small Point.*

uncommon. Few people considered photography art, and even fewer collected it. Most amateurs were forgotten because there were few avenues by which to make their work known. Aside from photography exhibits and occasional appearances in Bath newspapers, Emma's photographs went largely unseen. She did give them to family and friends as gifts, but she never sold them commercially.

The loss of Emma's photographs from public view for so many years does not diminish their significance today, however. Photography has always been associated with preserving history. "The photographer's punctilio," writes Berenice Abbott, "is his recognition of the *now*—to see it so clearly that he looks through it to the past and senses the future." As a documentarian, Emma did this extraordinarily well. Like contemporary photographer Paul Strand, she captured subjects that "in their ordinariness are extraordinarily representative," and in doing so she captured history. "If the living take that history upon themselves," writes art critic John Berger in *About Looking*, "if the past becomes an integral part of the process of people making their own history, then photographs would reacquire a living context, they would continue to exist in time, instead of being arrested moments." Taking this idea one step further, Berger points out that if photographs do continue to exist in time, "The distinction between the private and public uses of photography would be transcended," and at that point, "The Family of Man would exist."

But it is Emma's artistic vision that I always return to. Her photographs, from the moment I first saw them, are a revelation to me.

The Photographs of Emma D. Sewall 1836–1919

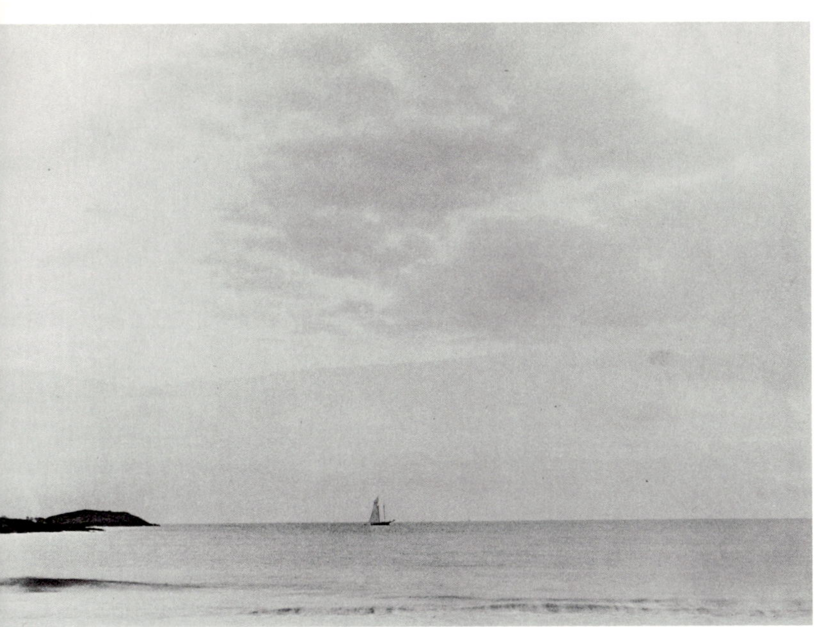

A Calm Morning from *The Rivers and Marshes of Small Point.*

Overhead a cloudless sky of intense blue, not a breath of wind to disturb the quiet—only in the distance the muffled unceasing roar of the sea. The solitude and desolation were complete and with a loneliness seldom experienced we turned back to the haunts of men, feeling almost that we had come back from the netherworld—even though we had left it filled with sunshine instead of shade.

from *The Rivers and Marshes of Small Point*

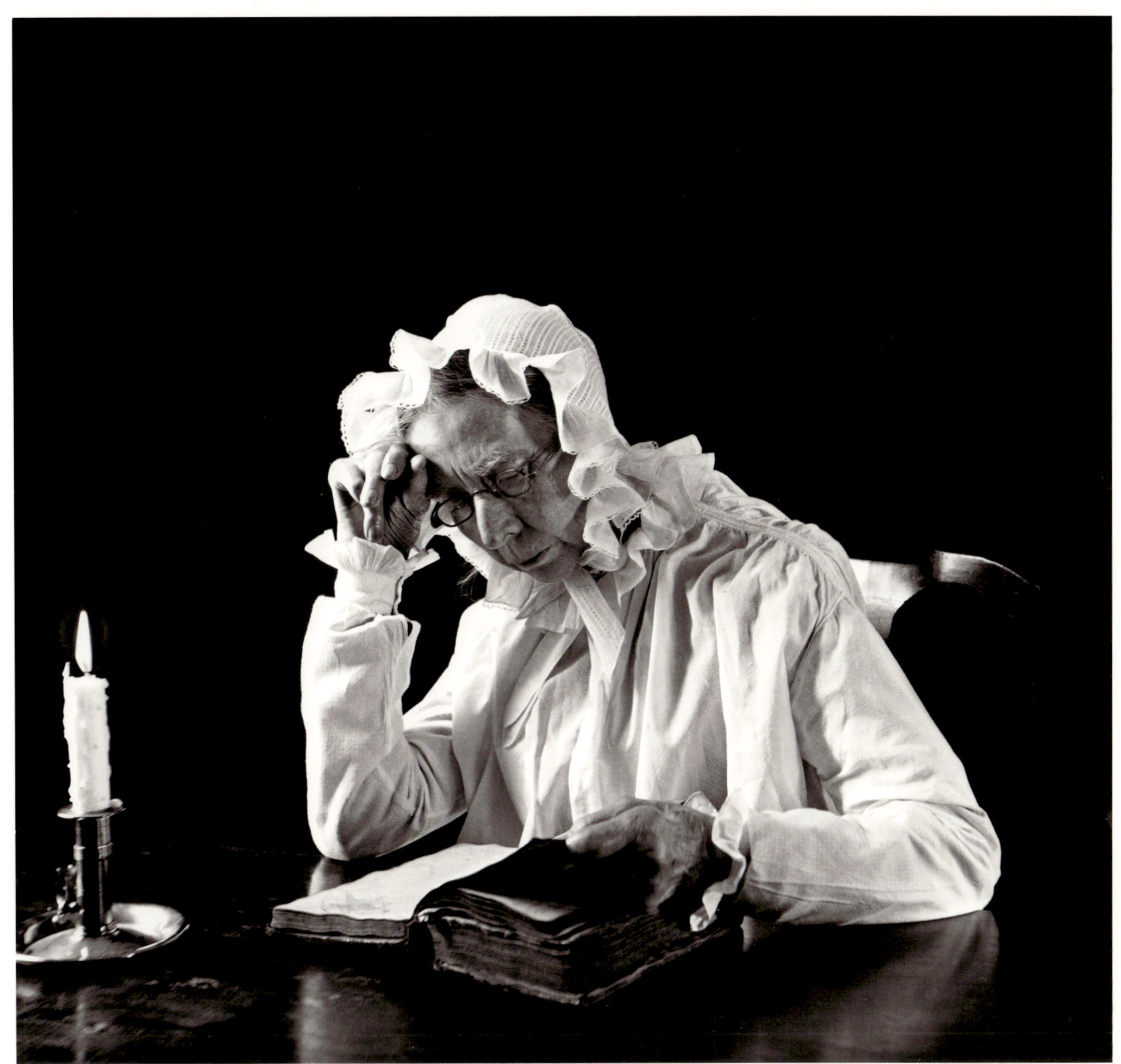

1. *When The Day's Work Is Done*

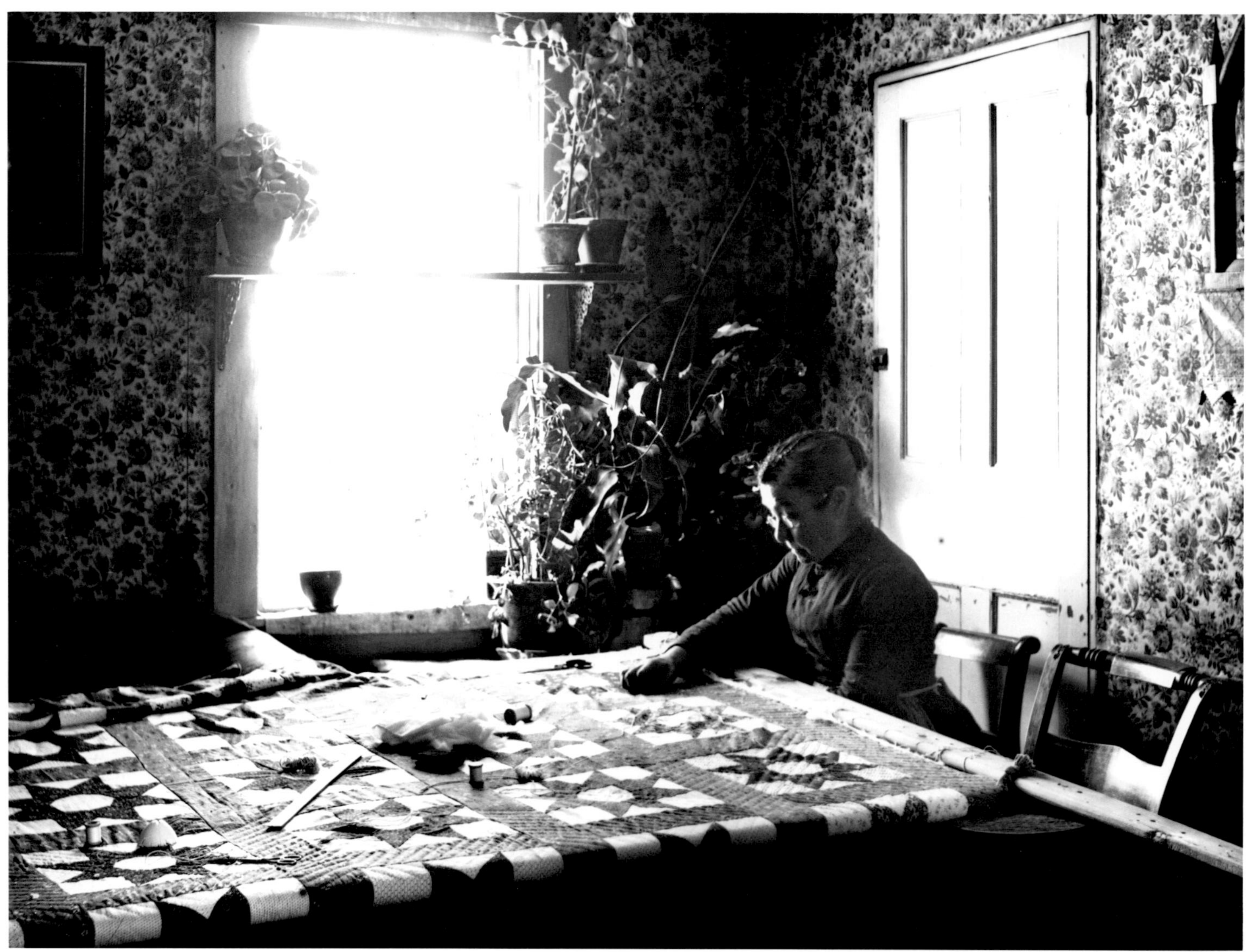

2. *Untitled*

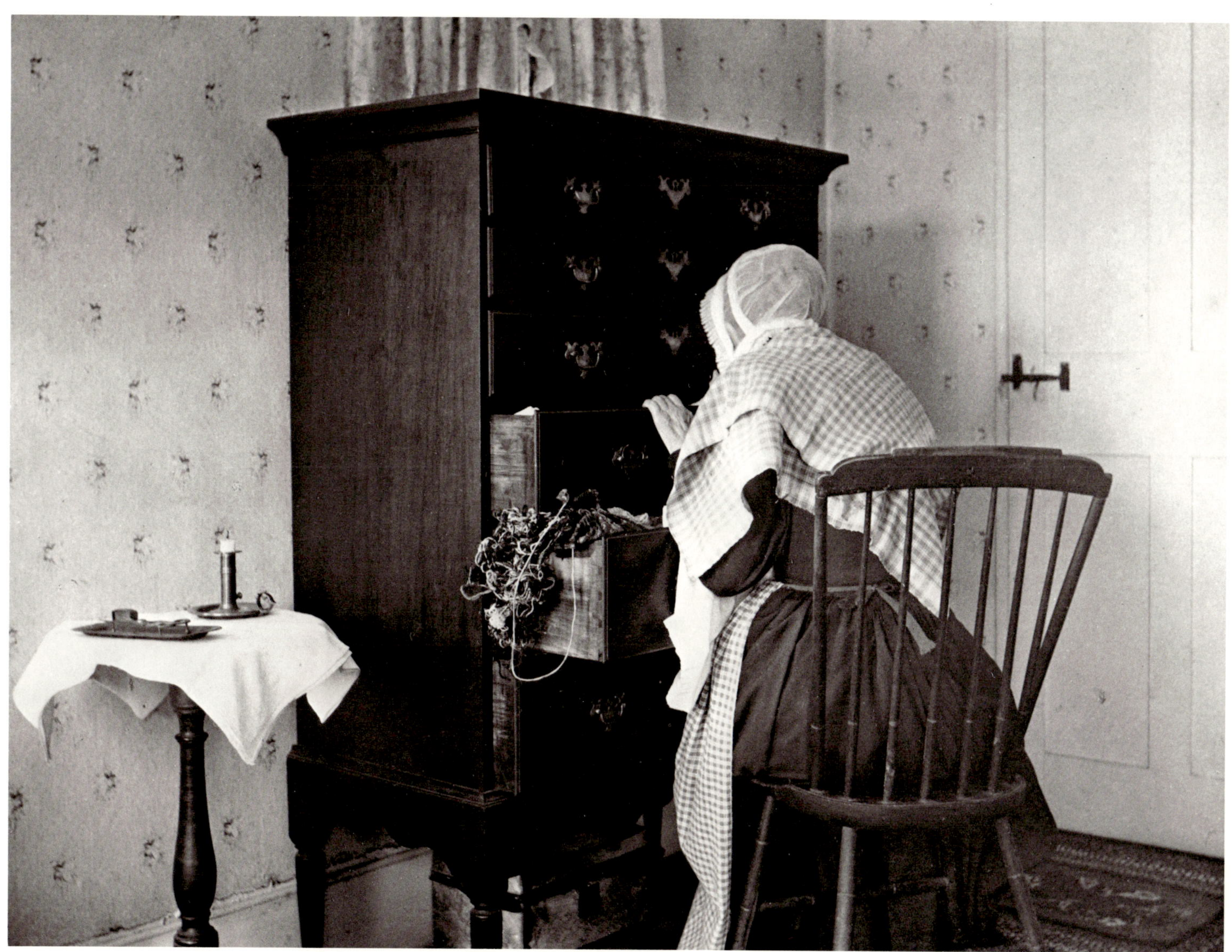

3. The Search

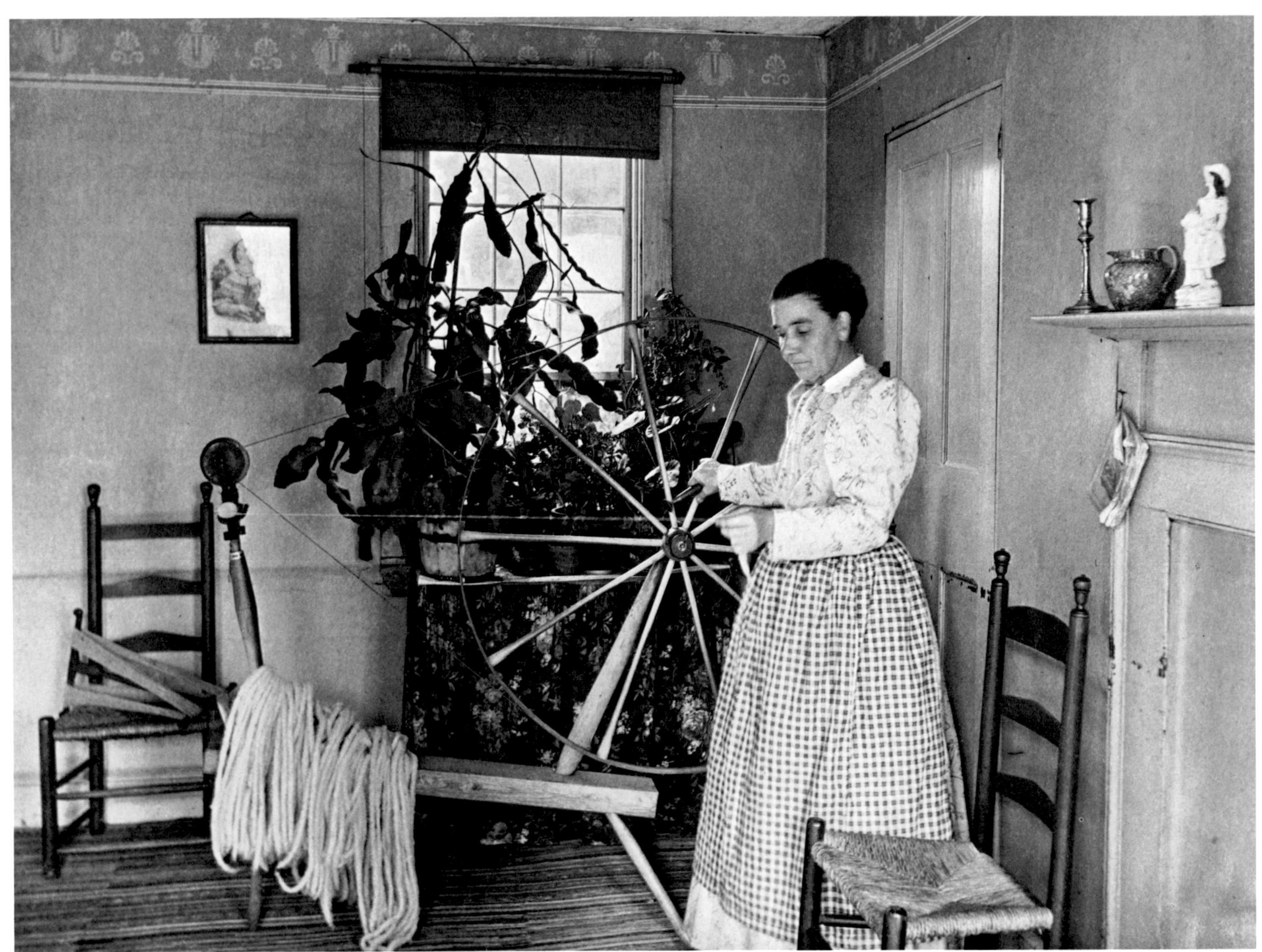

4. *Mrs. Young*

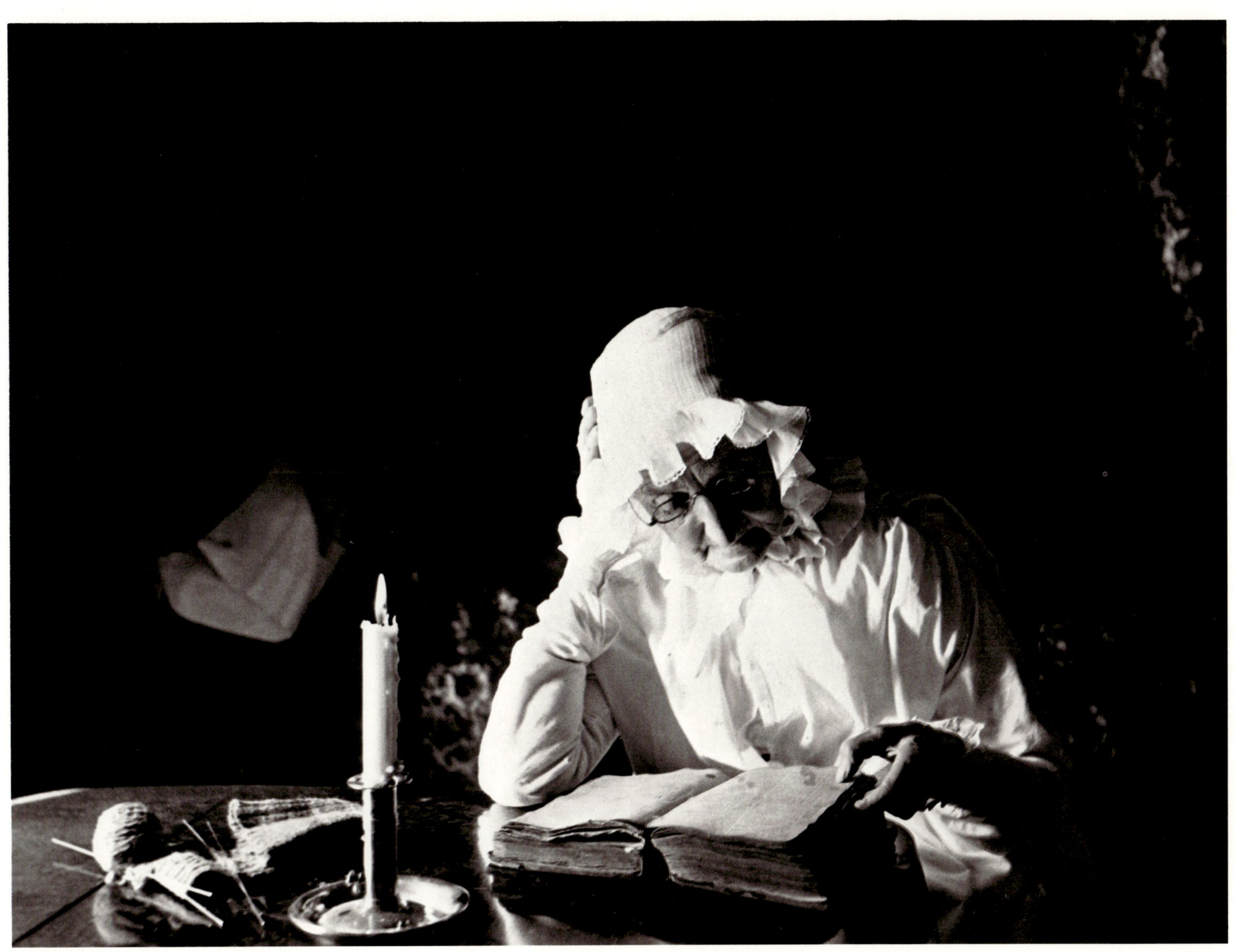

5. *Study for Miss Wilkins*

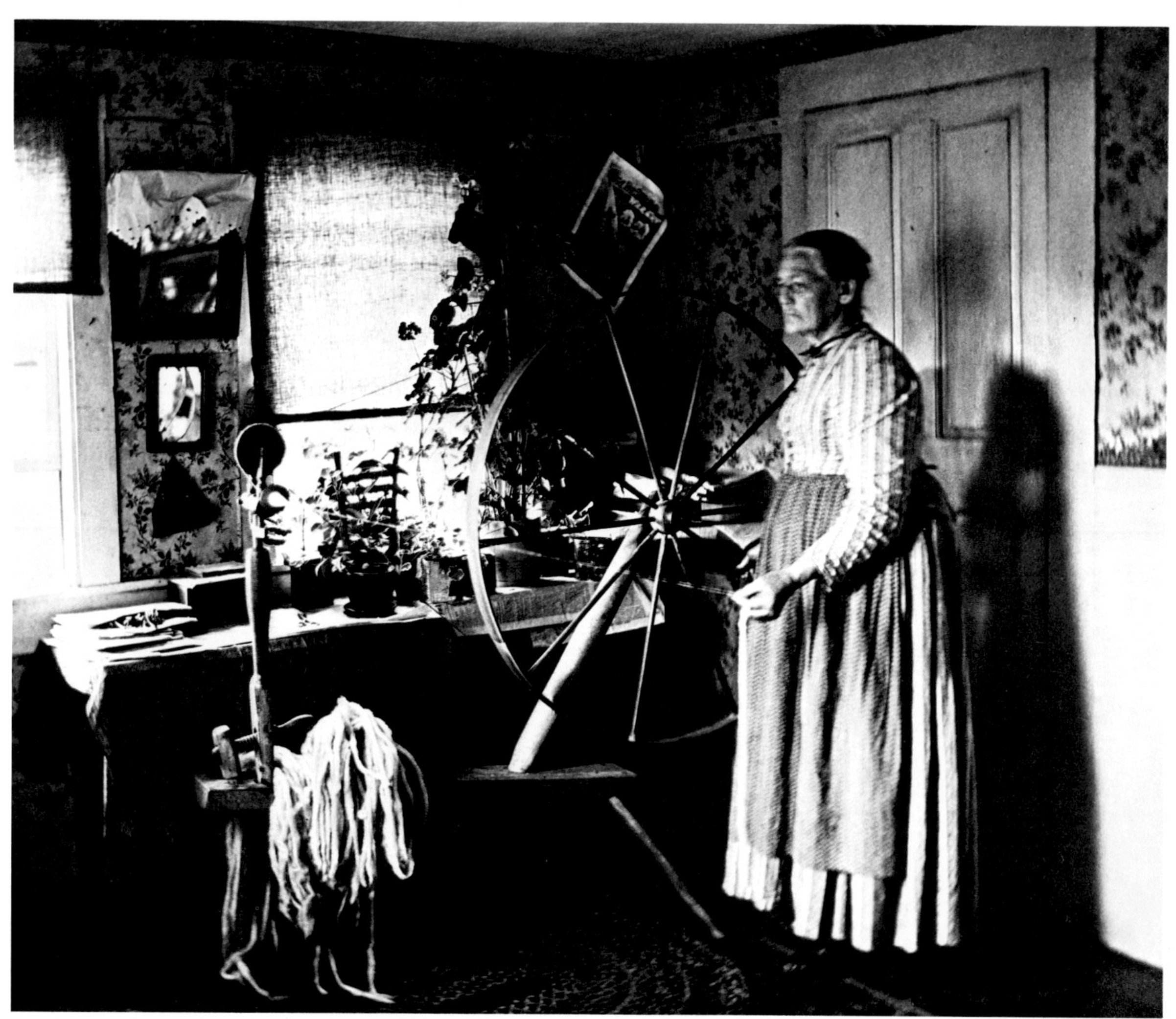

6. Mrs. Coffee—Small Point

Life Insurance
Company
1894 APRIL 1894
SUN MON TUE WED THU FRI SAT
1 2 3 4 5 6 7
8 9 10 11 12 13 14
15 16 17 18 19 20 21
22 23 24 25 26 27 28
29 30
FITZPATRICK, General Agent
PORTLAND, ME

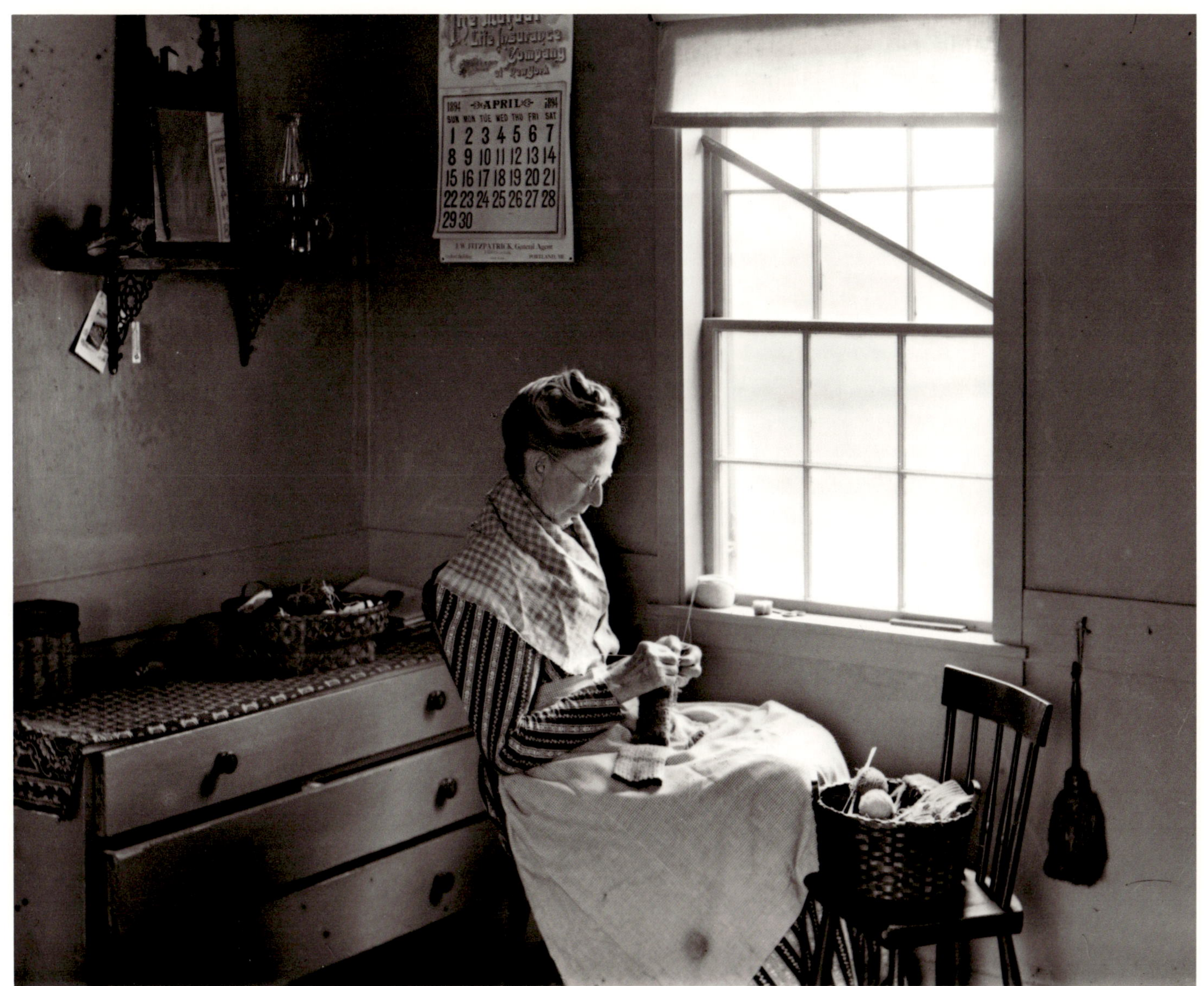

7. Untitled

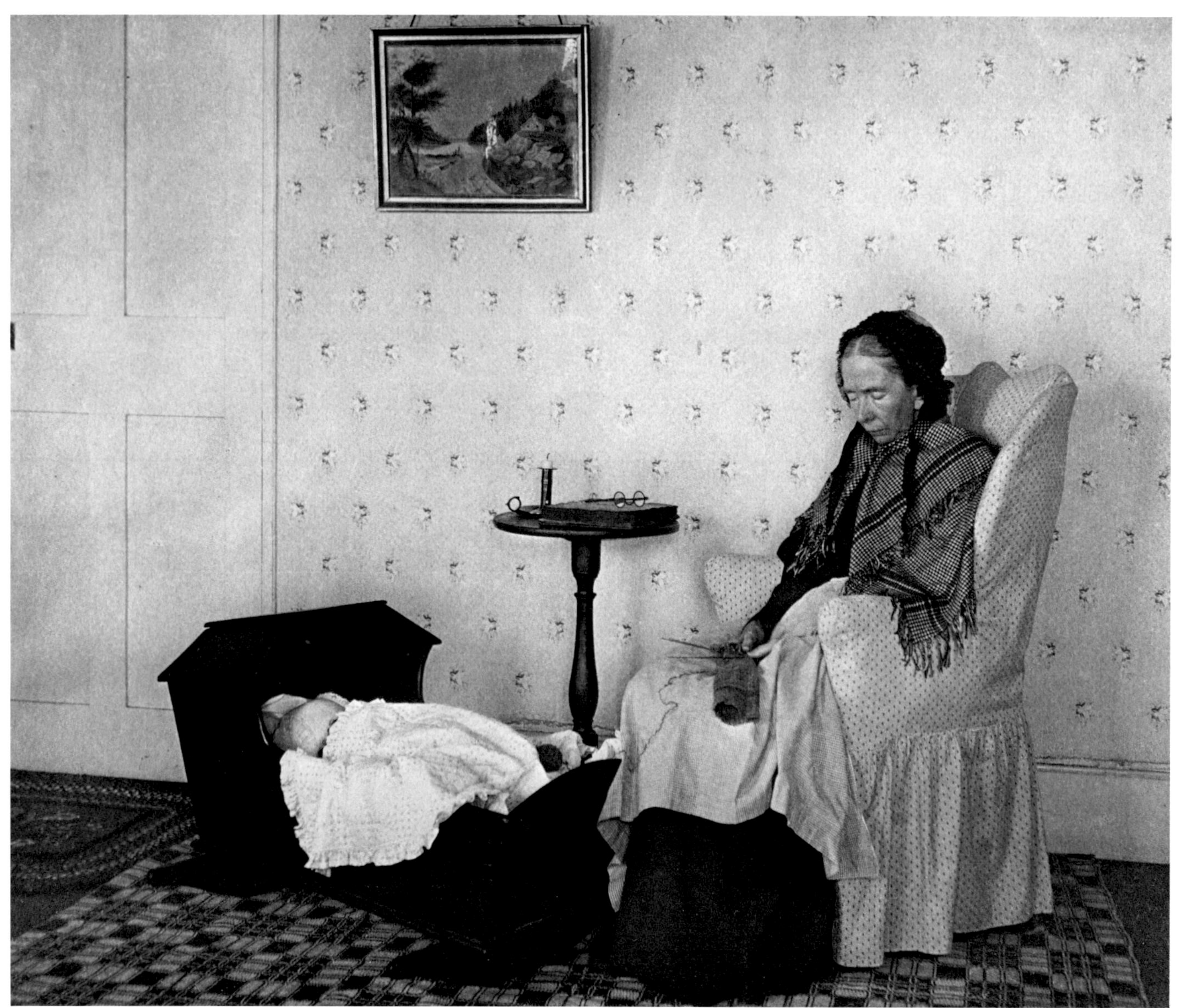

8. The Sleeping Grandmother

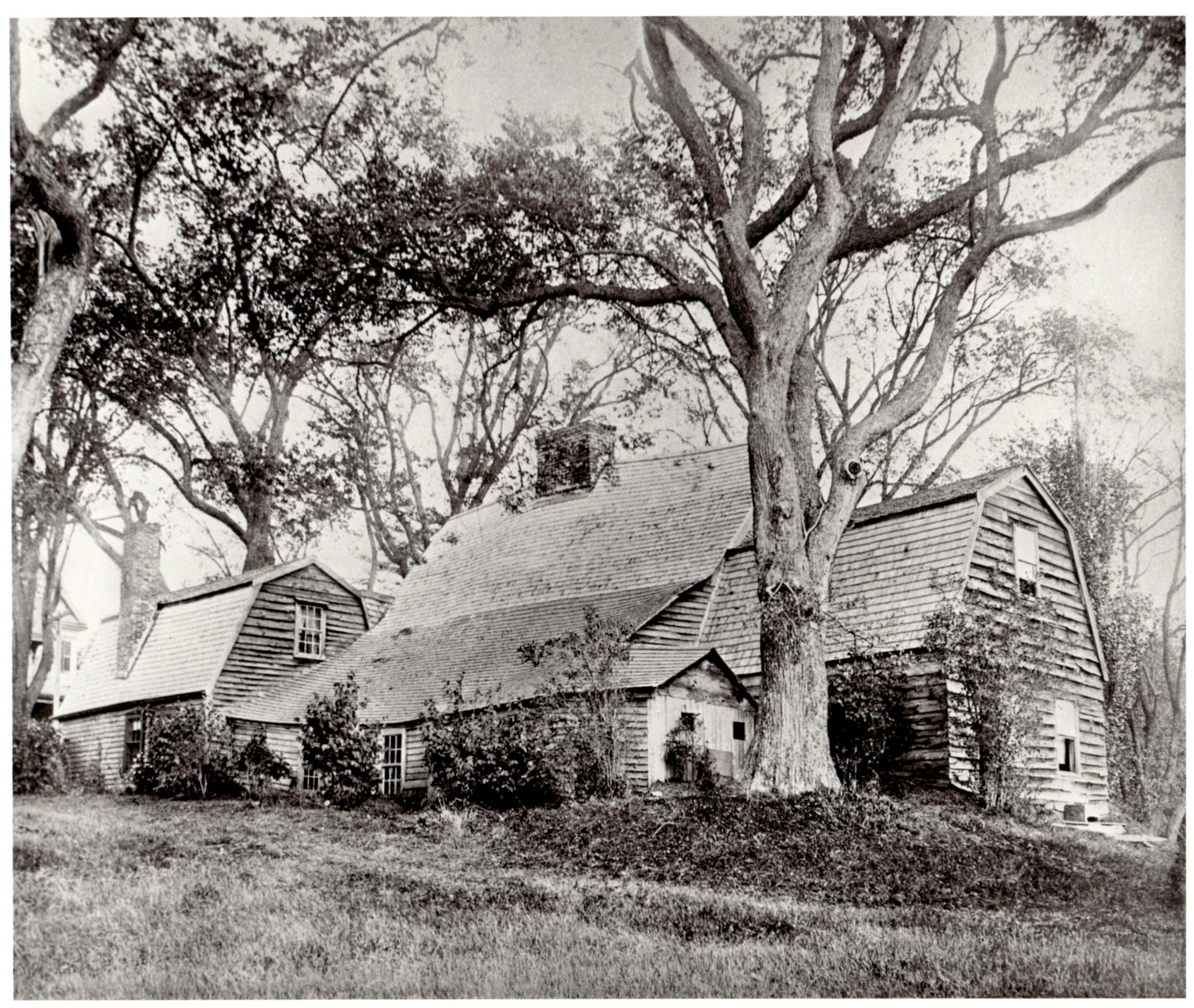

9. Fairbanks Homestead

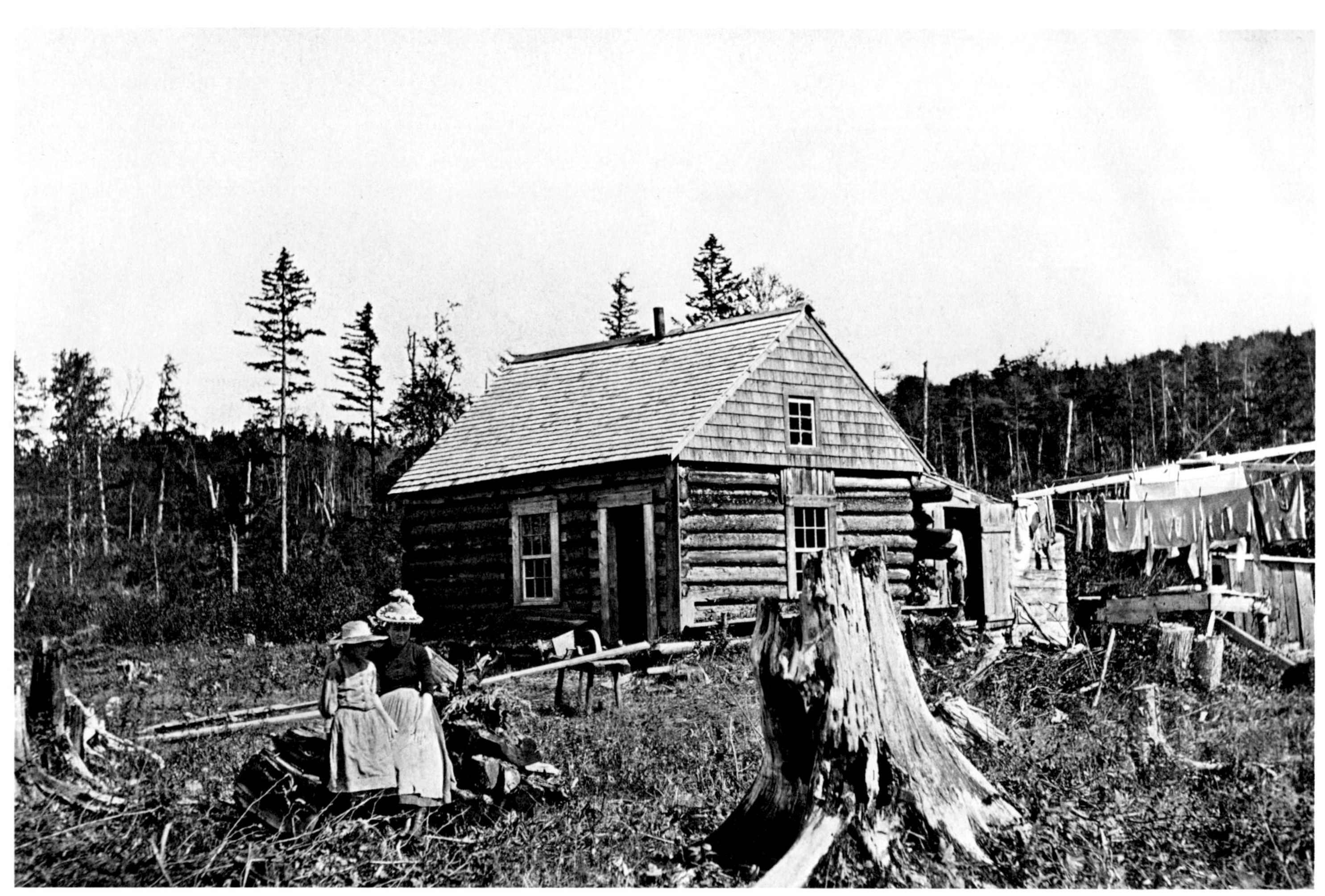

10. A Clearing Near Moosehead Lake

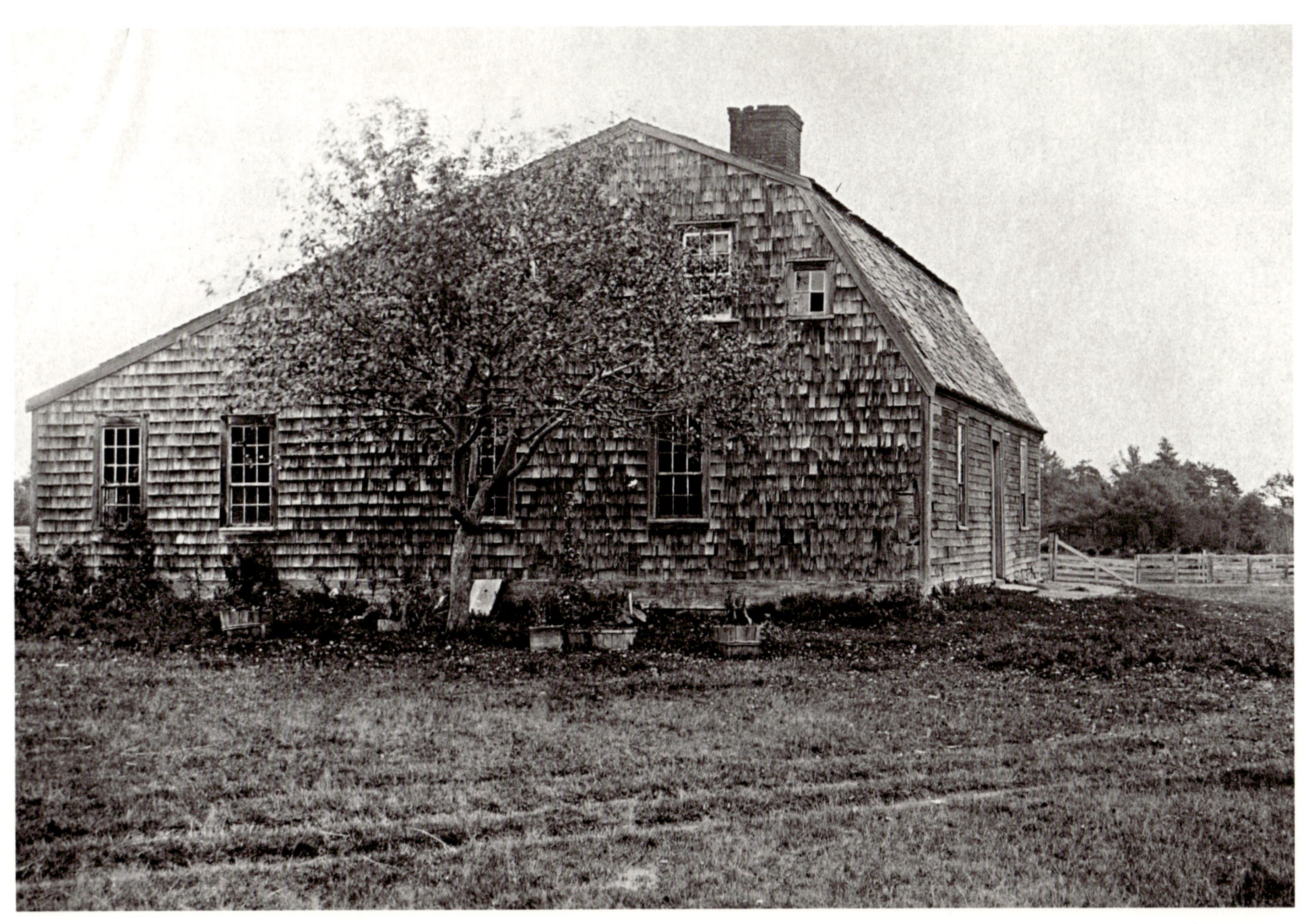

11. *Old House At New Meadows—Built 1762*

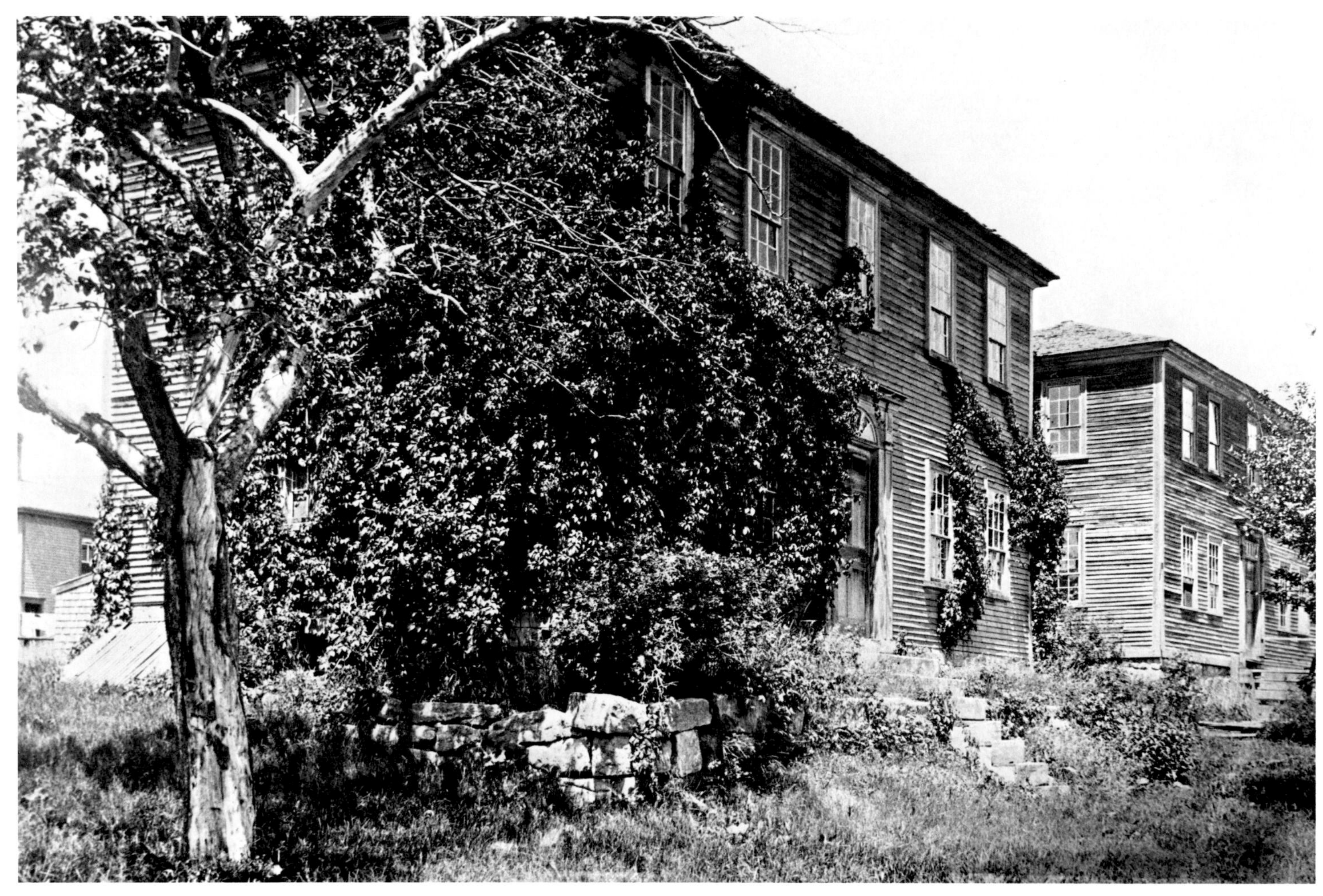

12. Corner of Pine and Washington Street

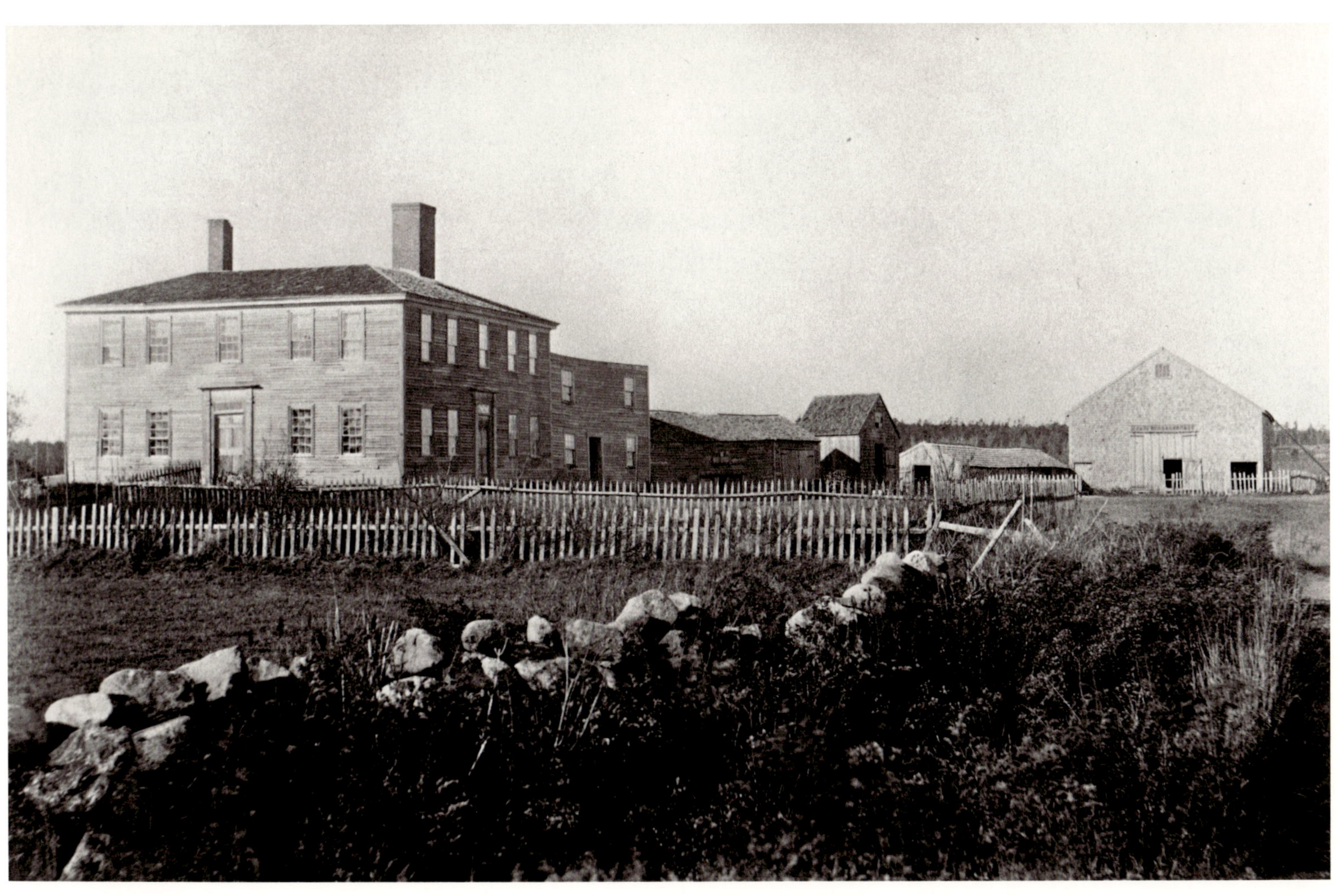

13. *Roger's House—Phippsburg 1887*

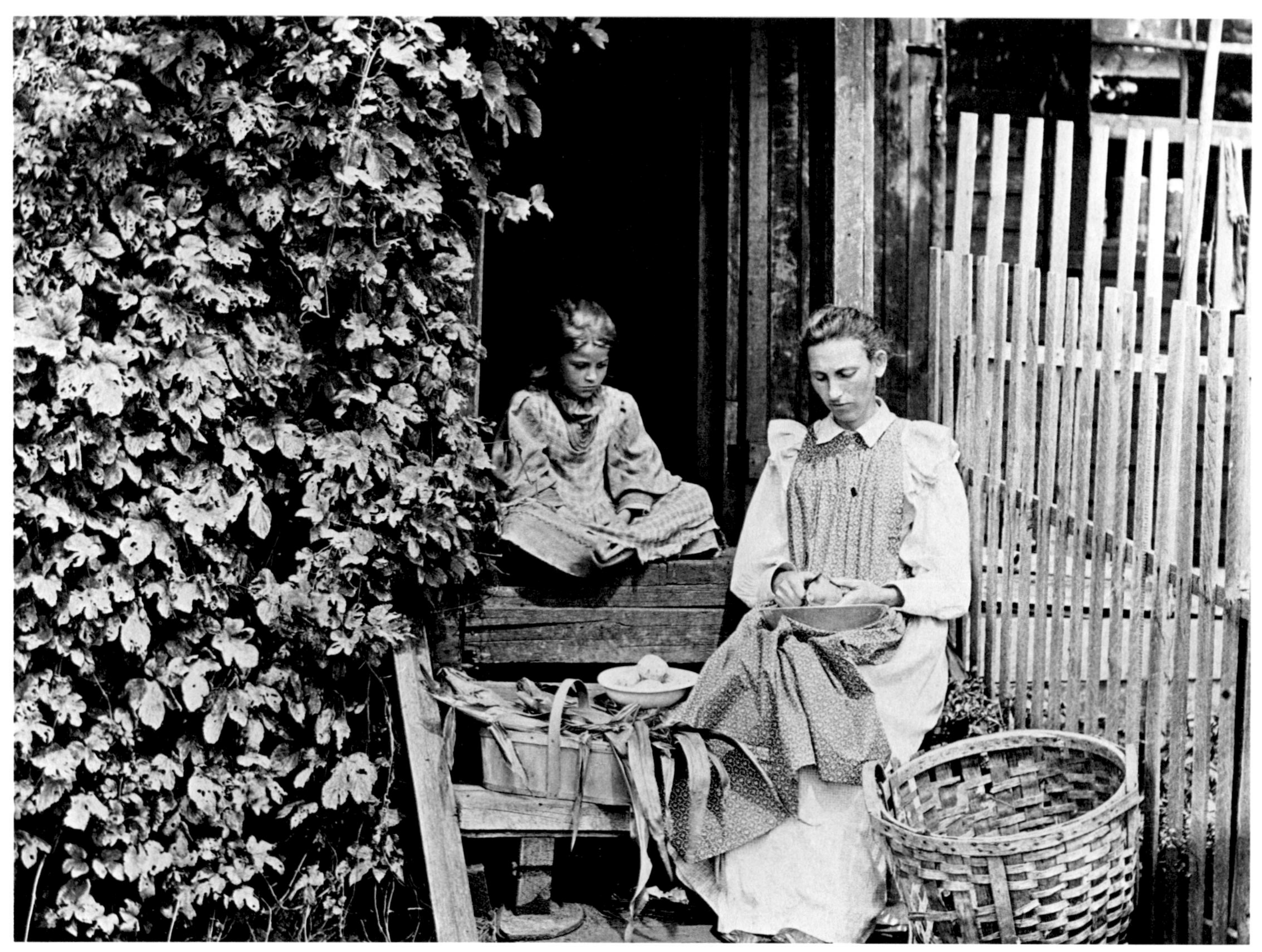

14. The Cottage Door

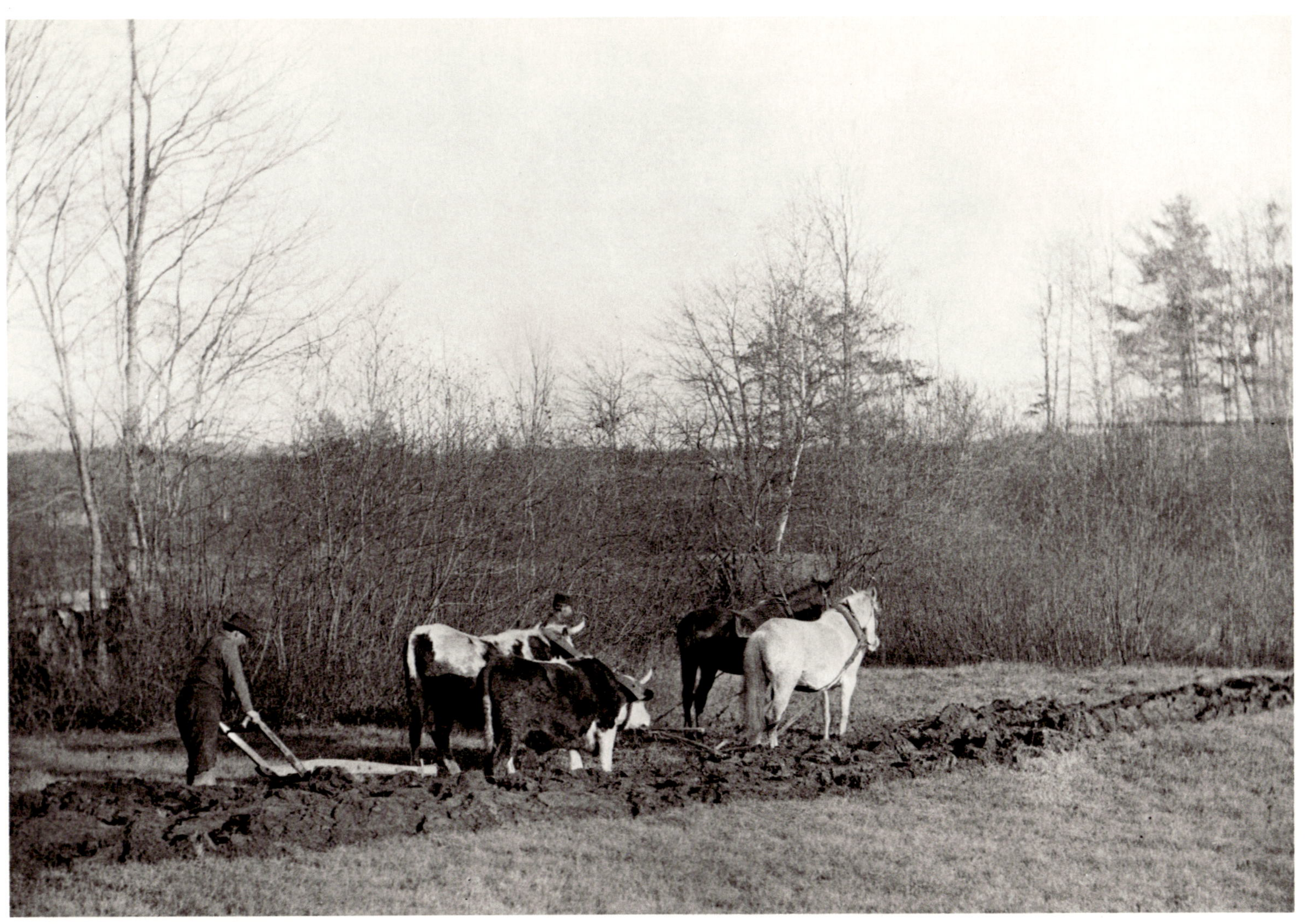

15. *Indian Summer—Near Topsham*

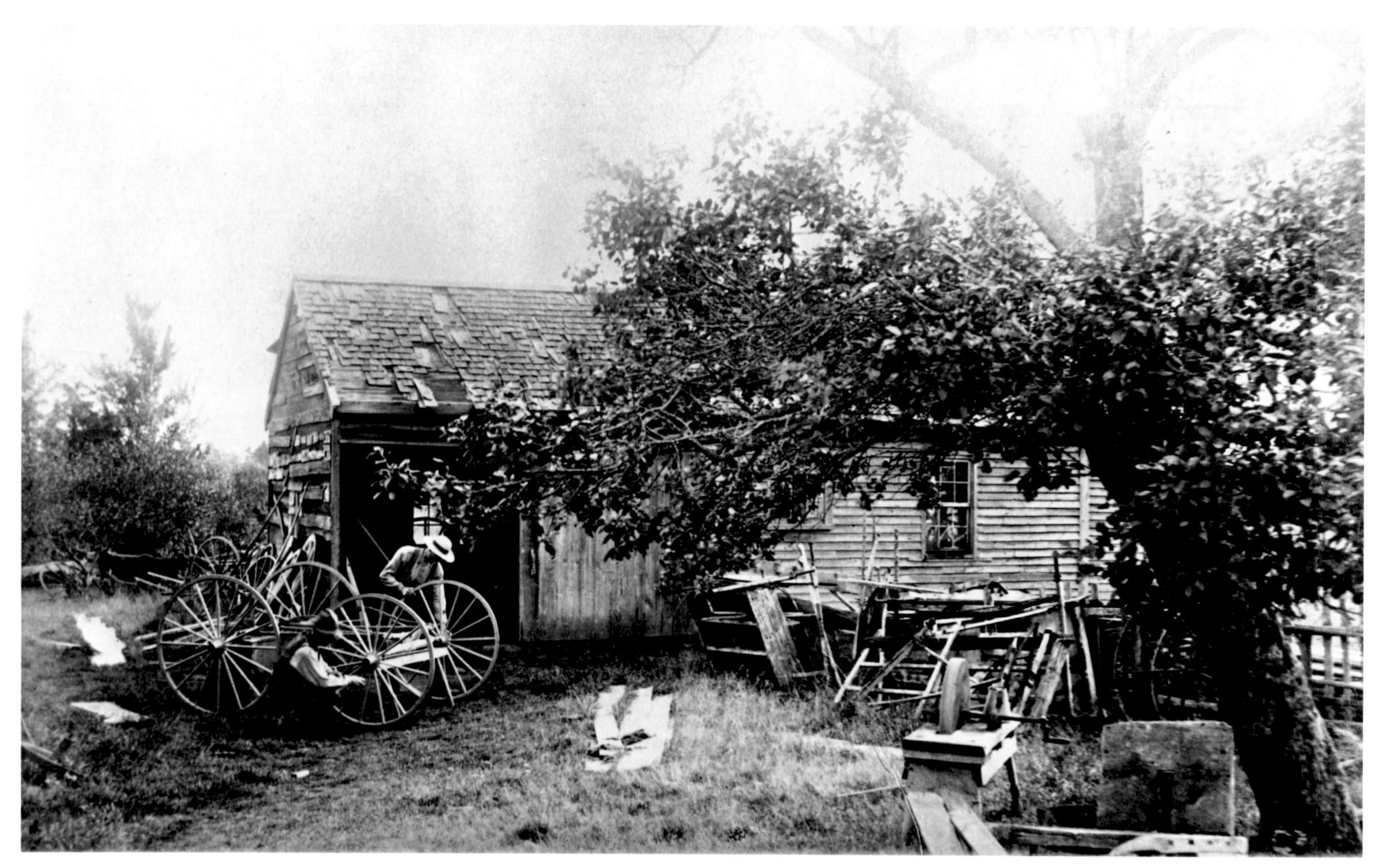

16. The Carriage Smith At Work—Harpswell Road 1888

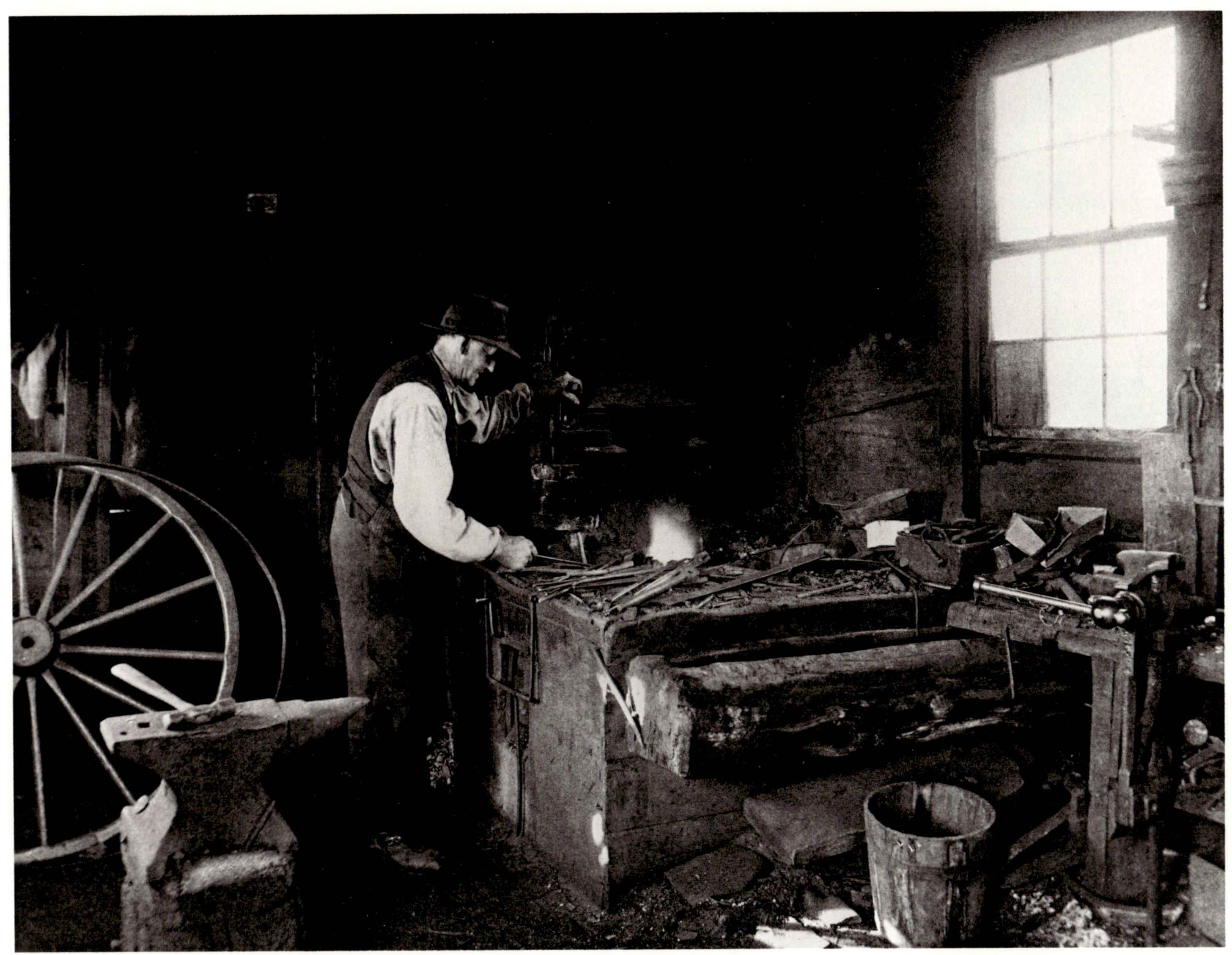

17. *The Village Blacksmith*

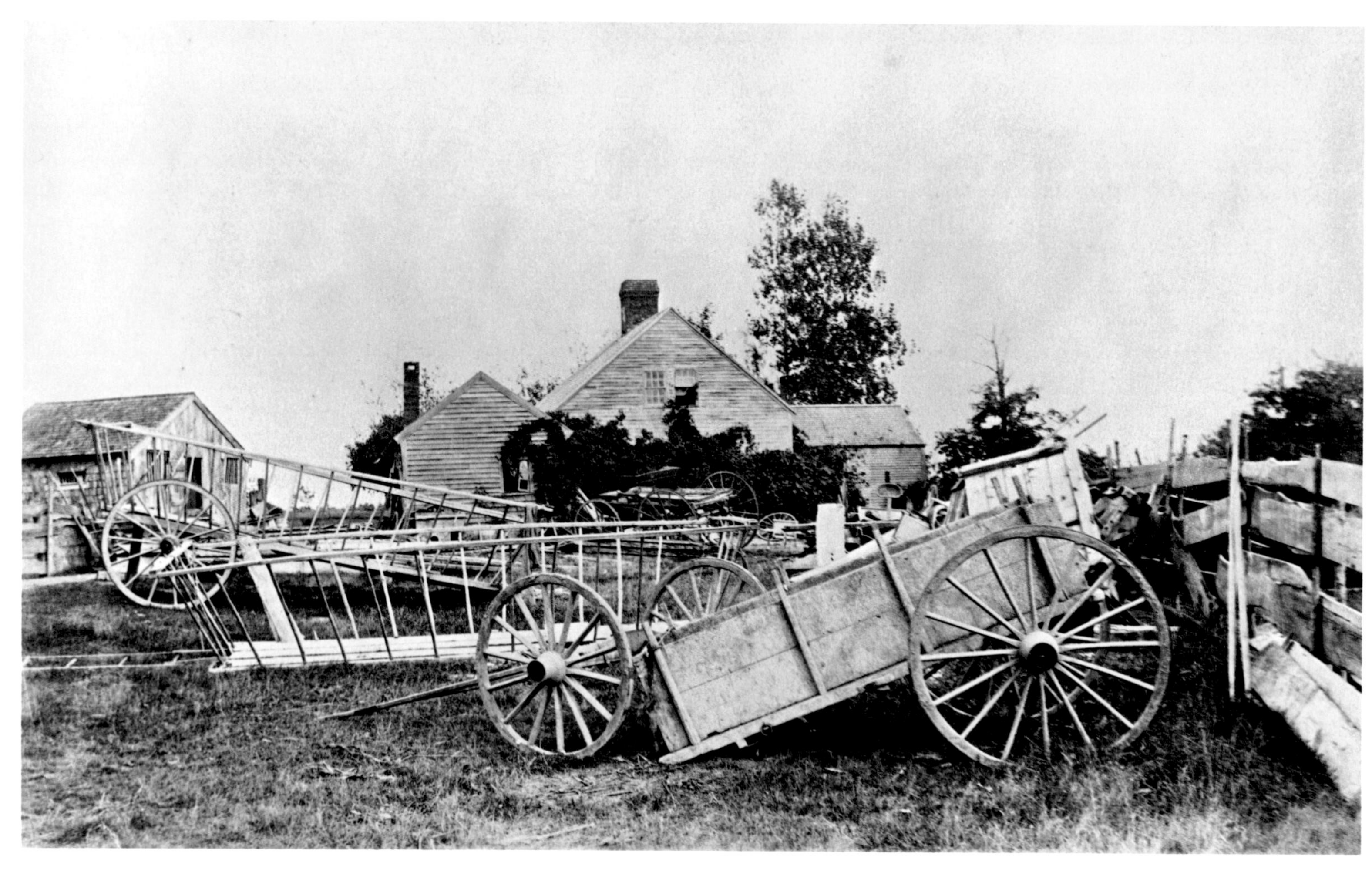

18. Home of the Country Carriage Smith—Harpswell Road 1888

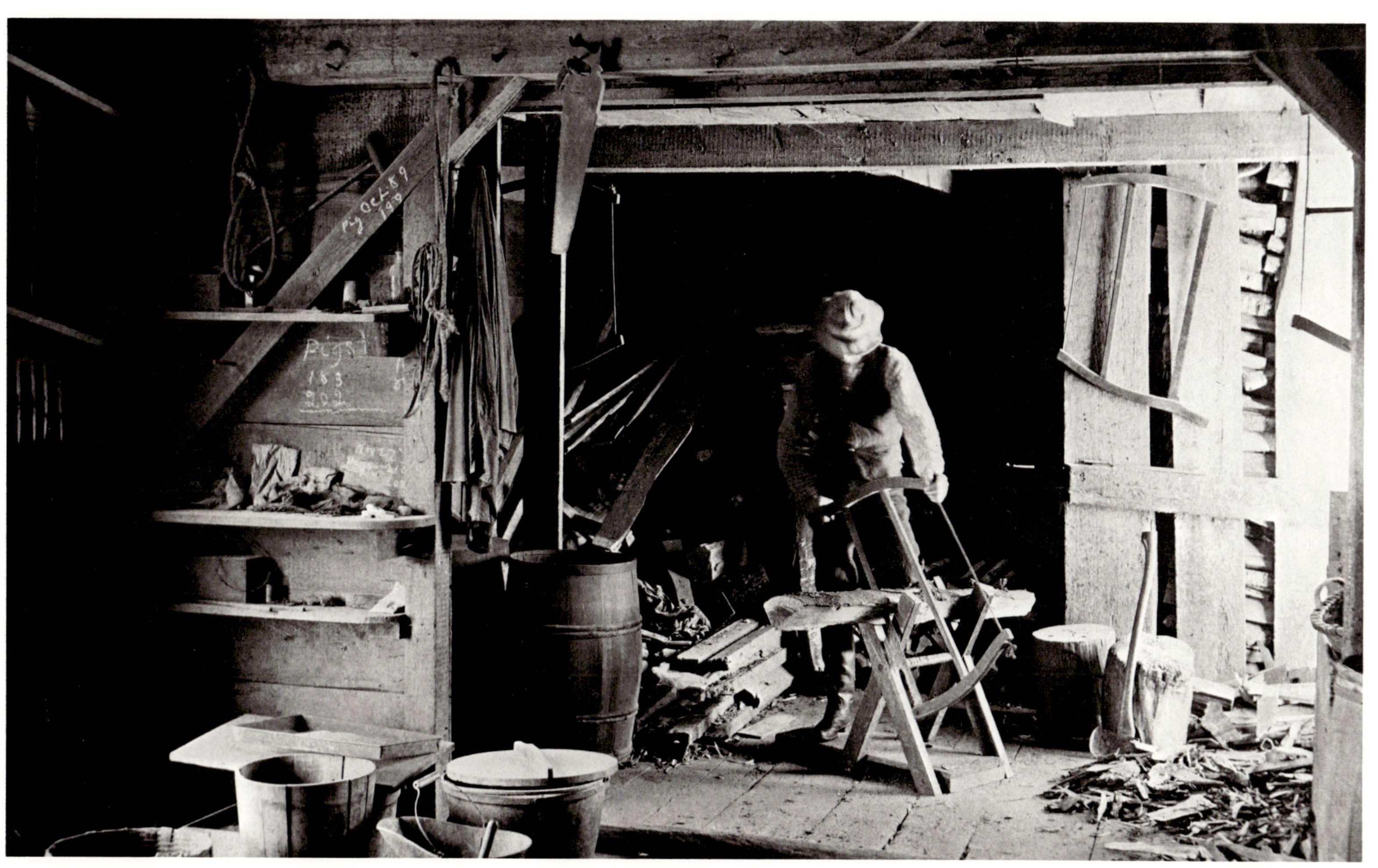

19. *Small Farmhouse Interior—1890*

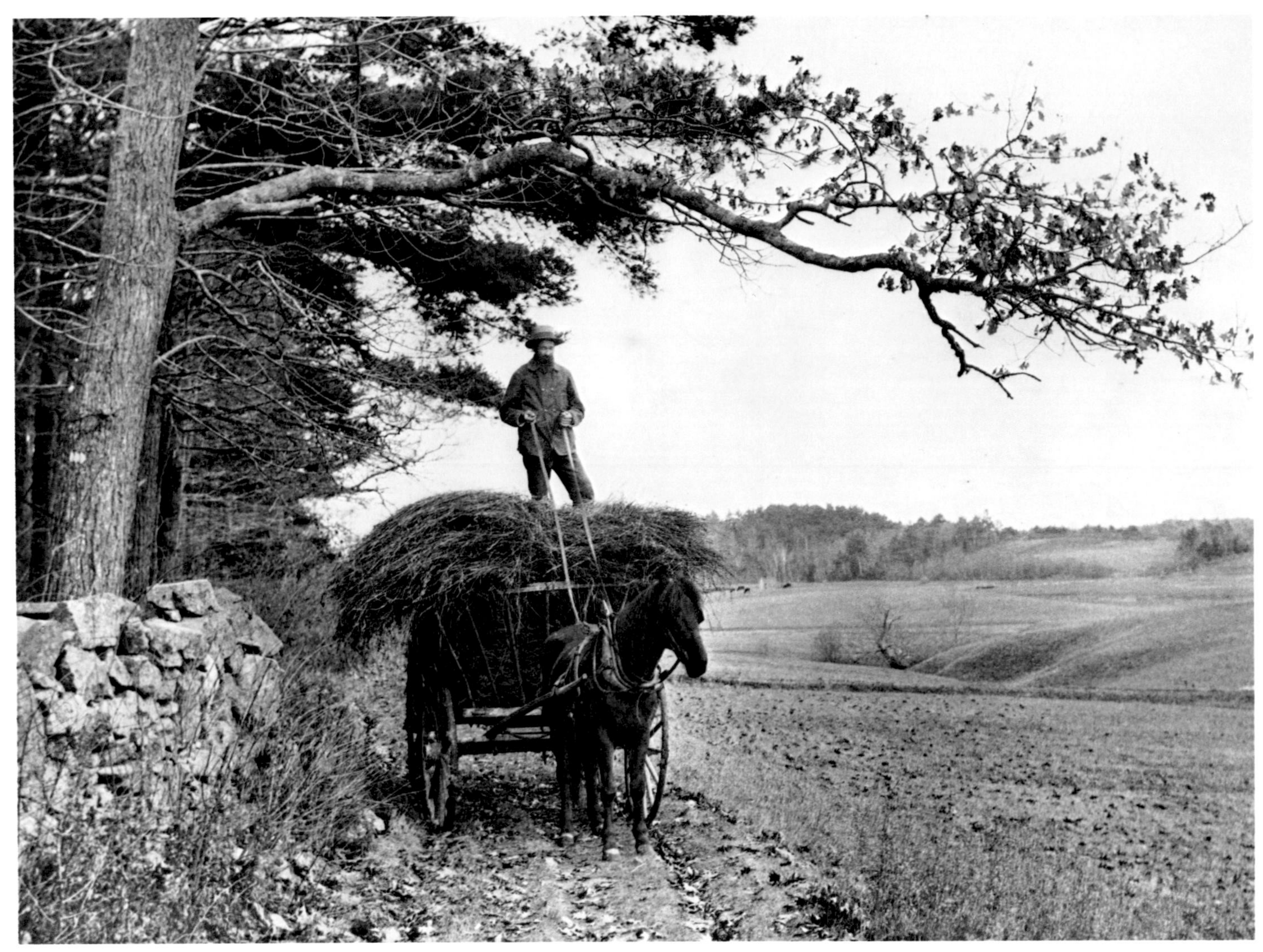

20. *Going To Market*

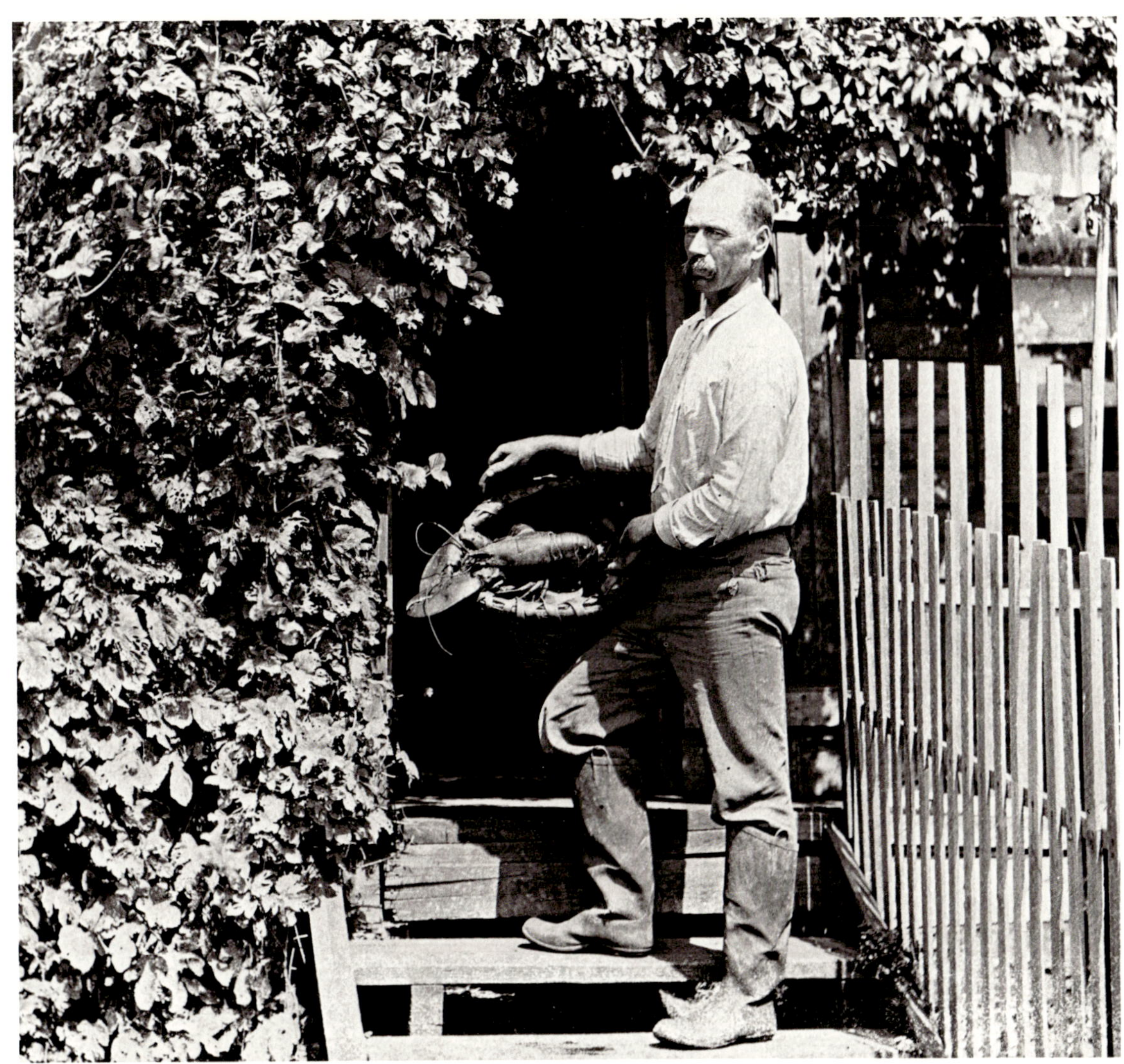

21. *The Lobsterman*

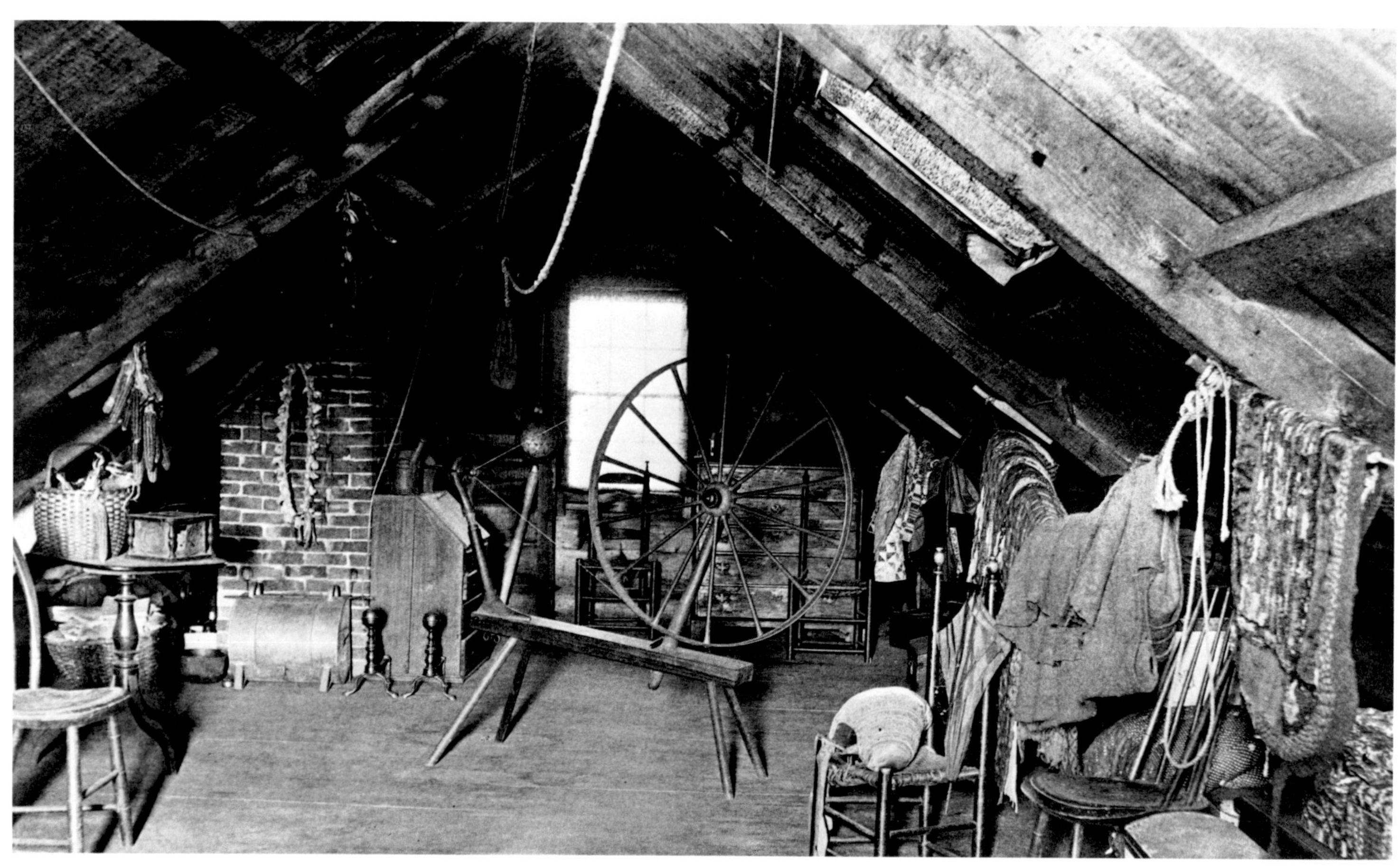

22. *The Garret—Sewall's Mills*

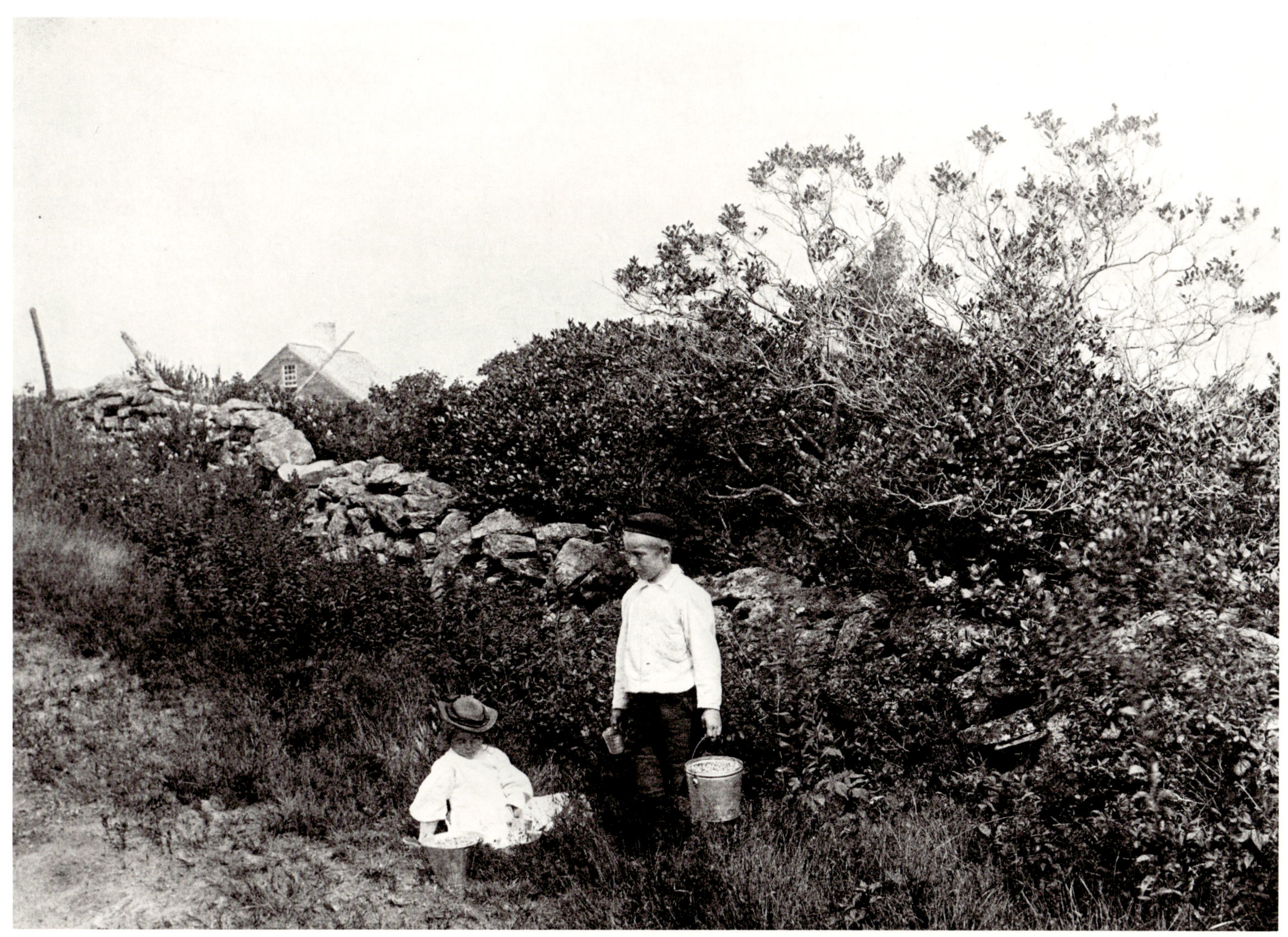

23. Blueberry Pickers

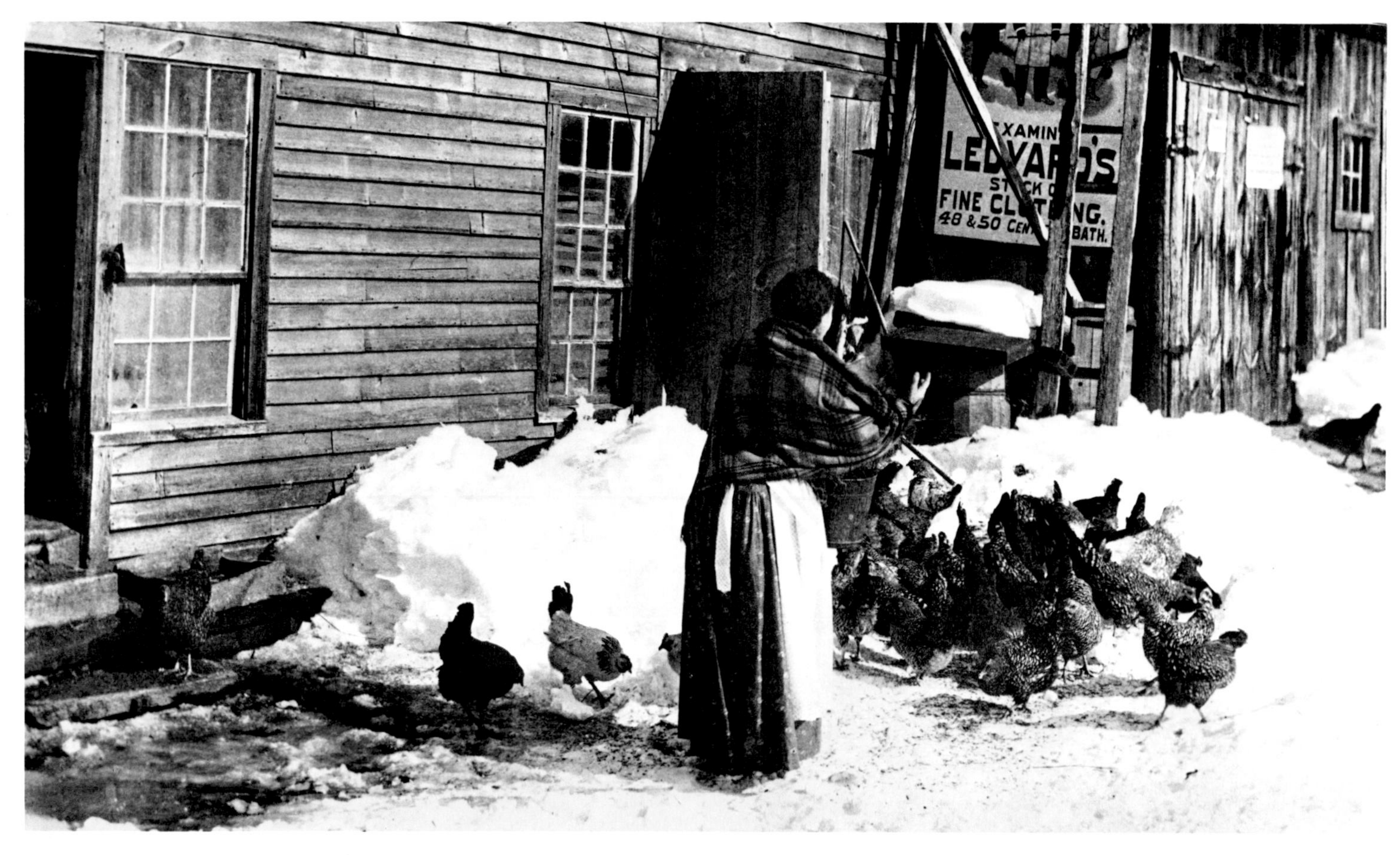

24. Feeding The Hens

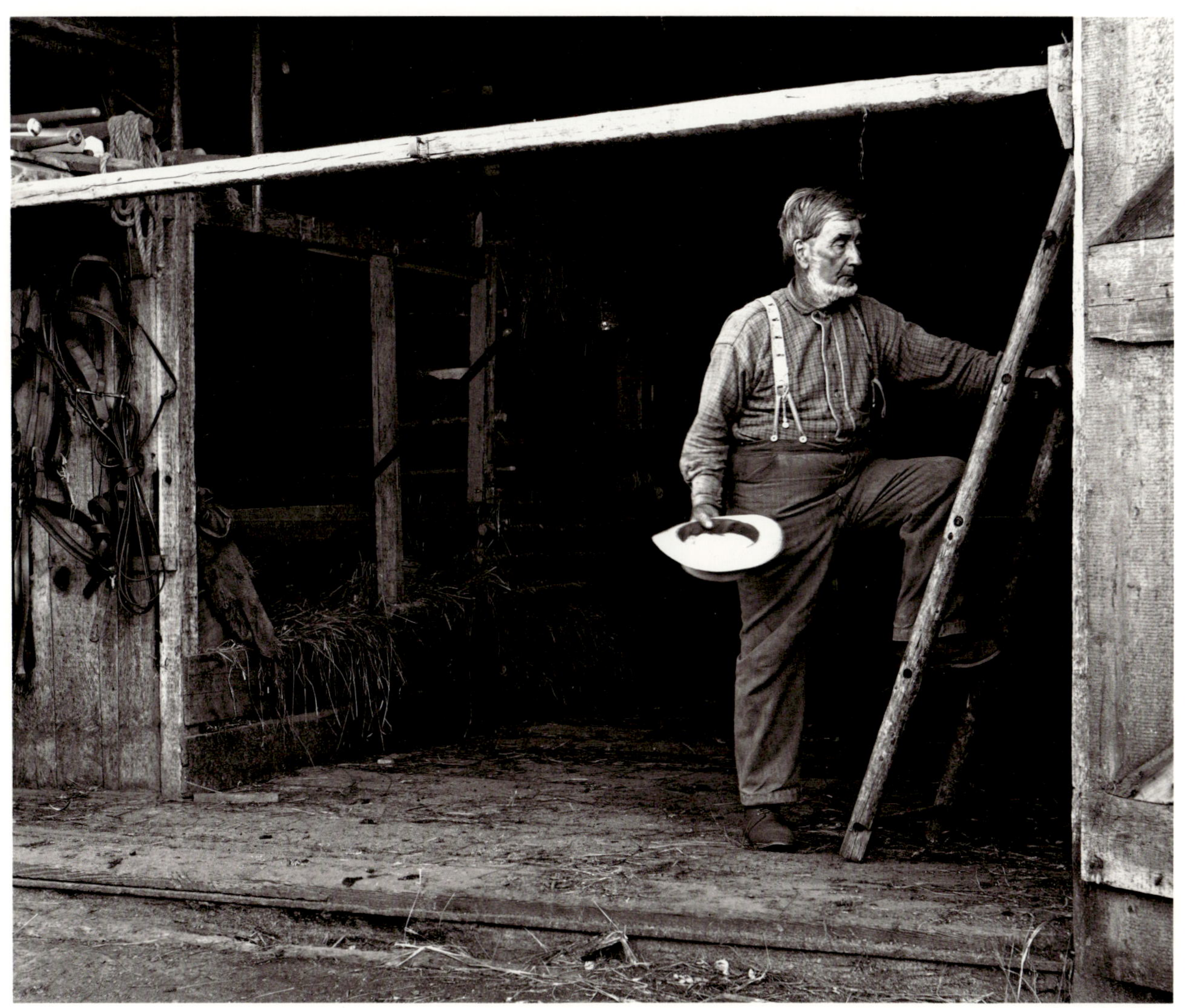

25. *Untitled*

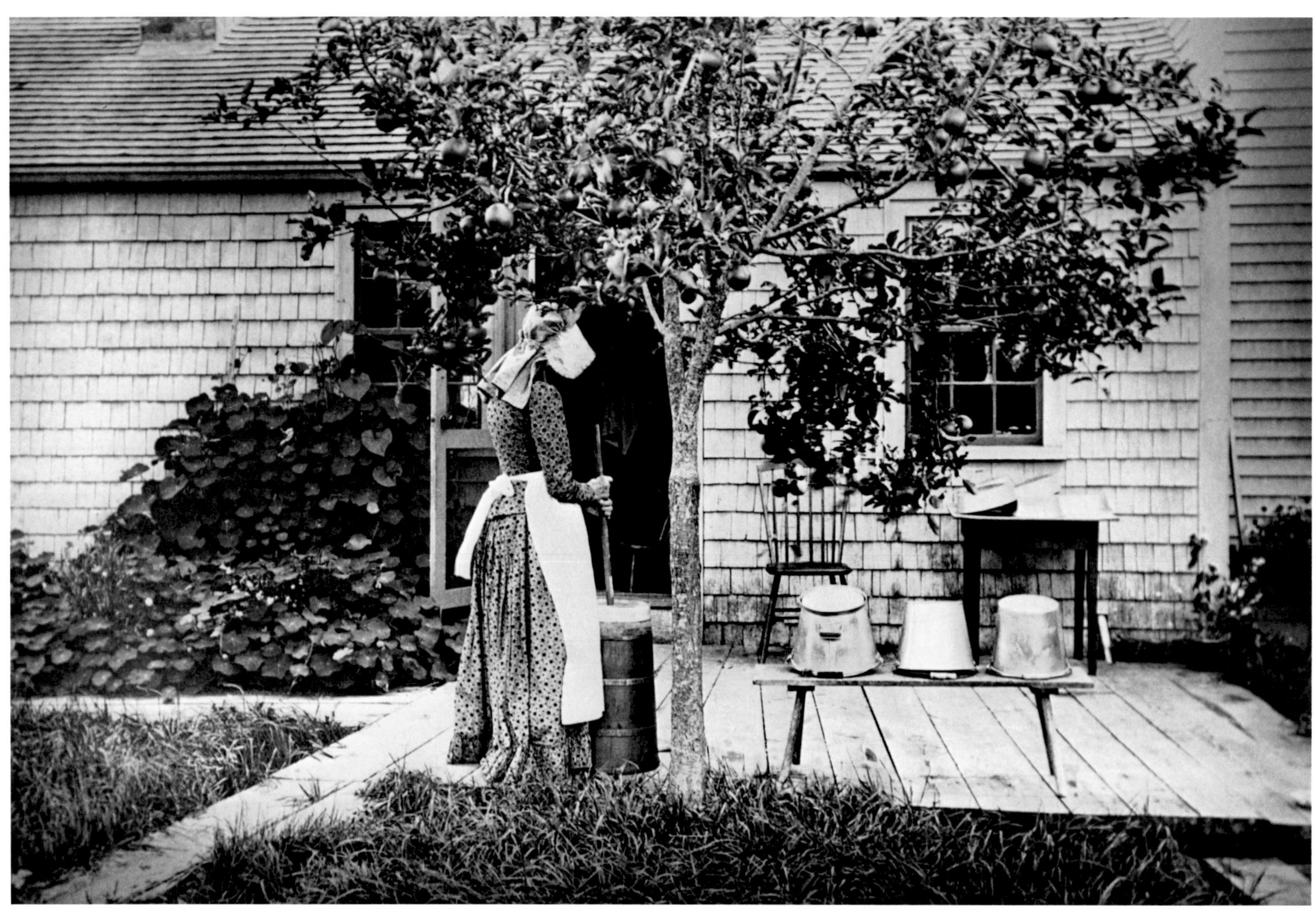

26. Untitled

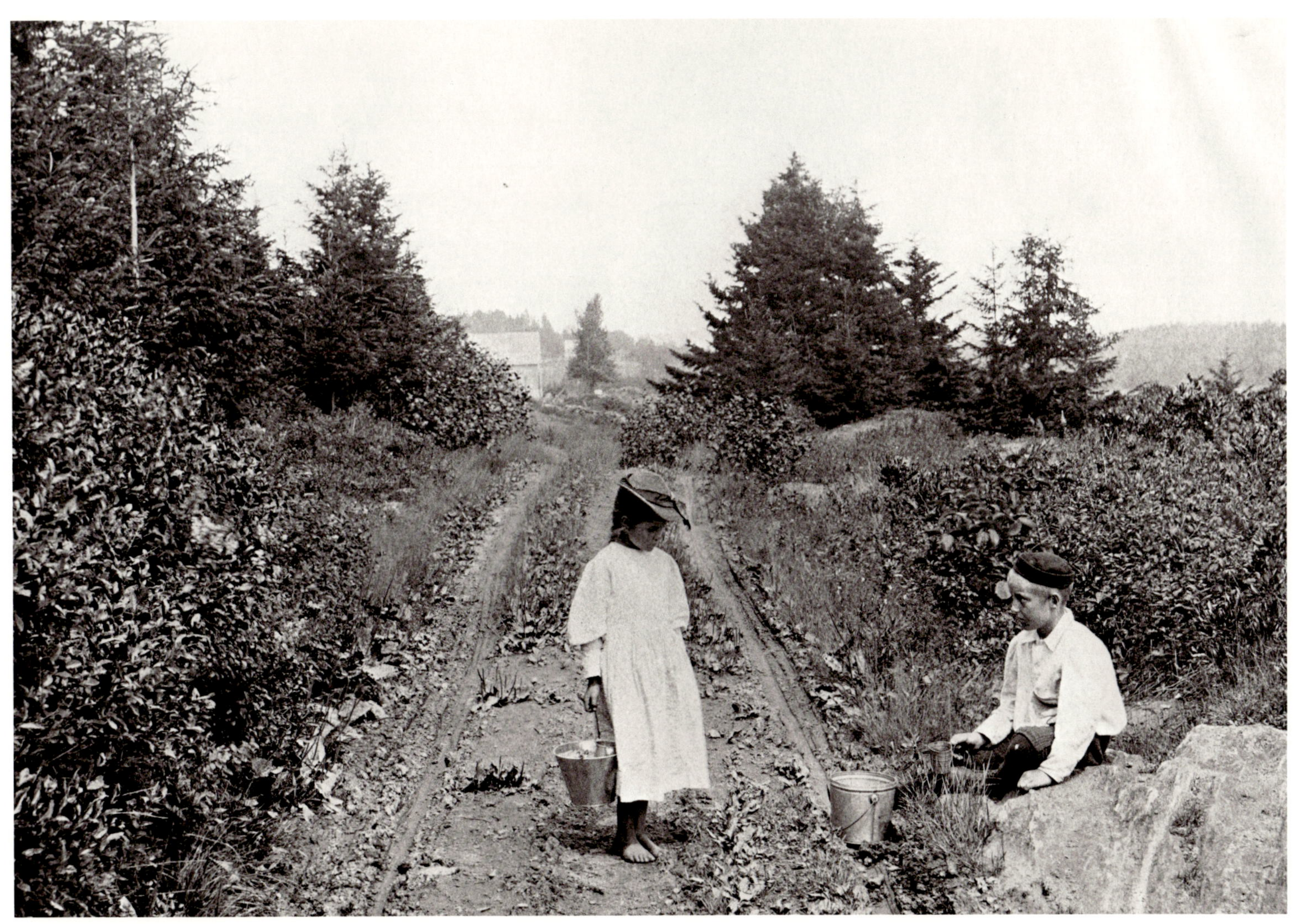

27. *Blueberry Pickers*

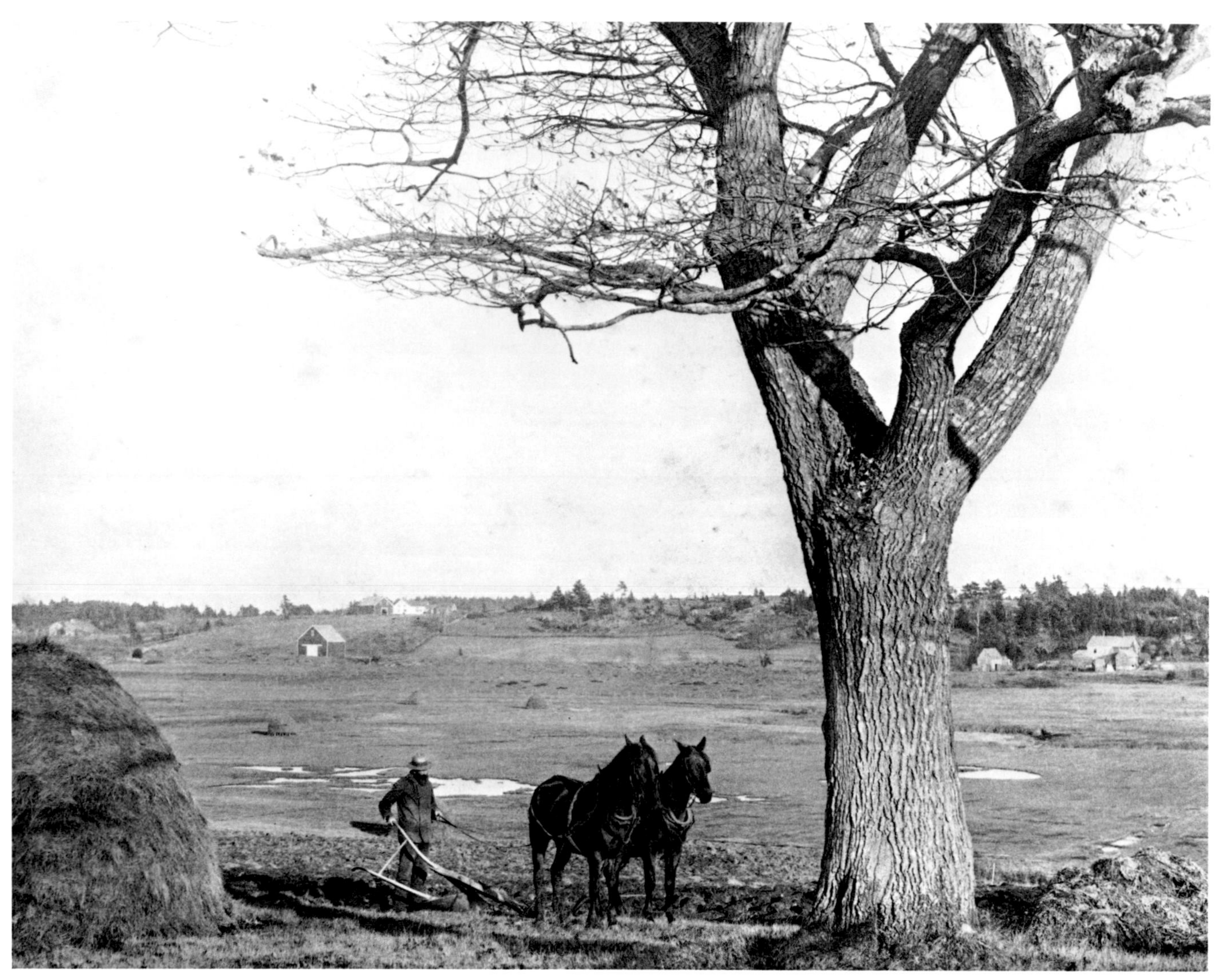

28. Autumn Ploughing

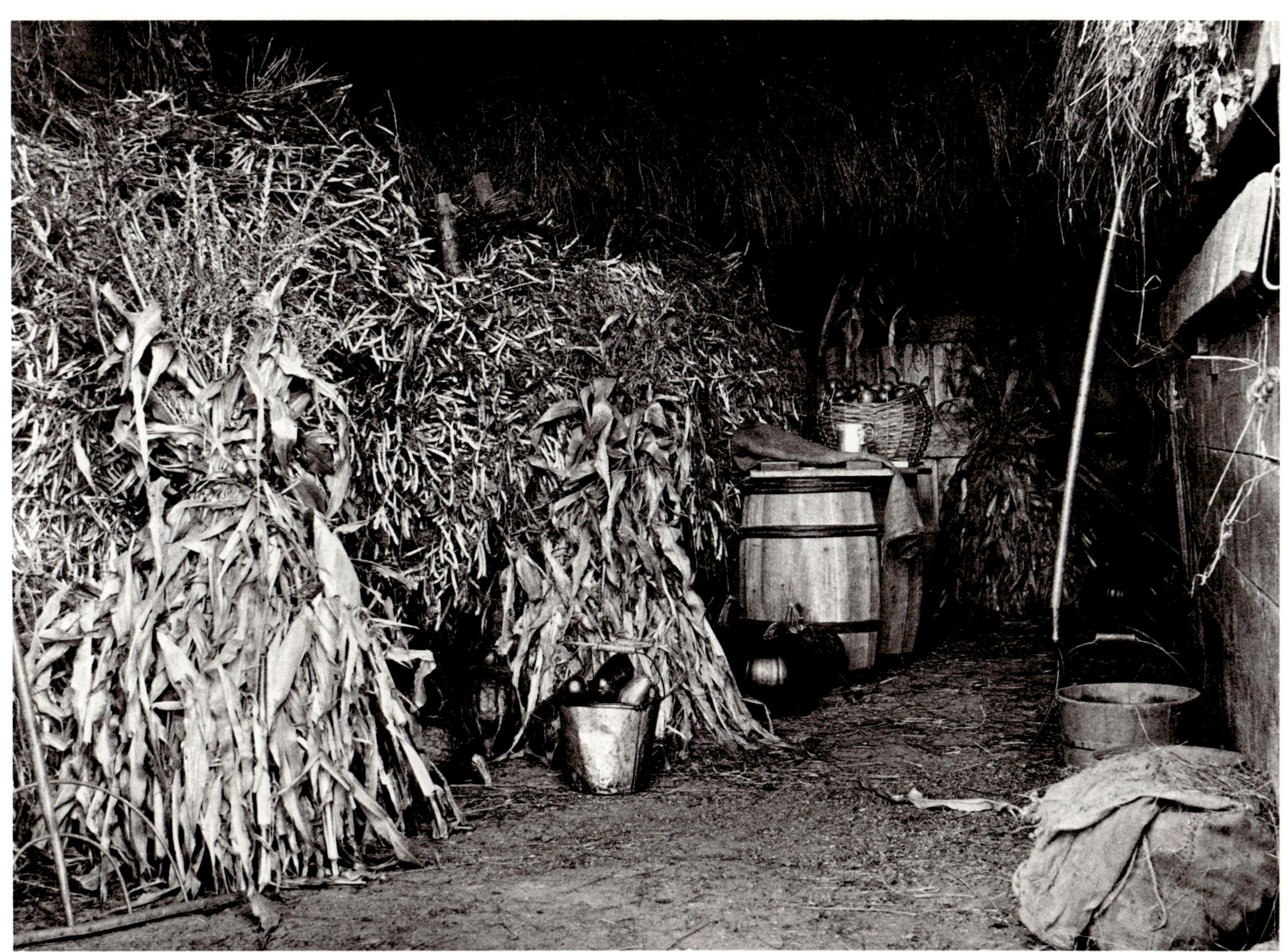

29. *Harvest Time*

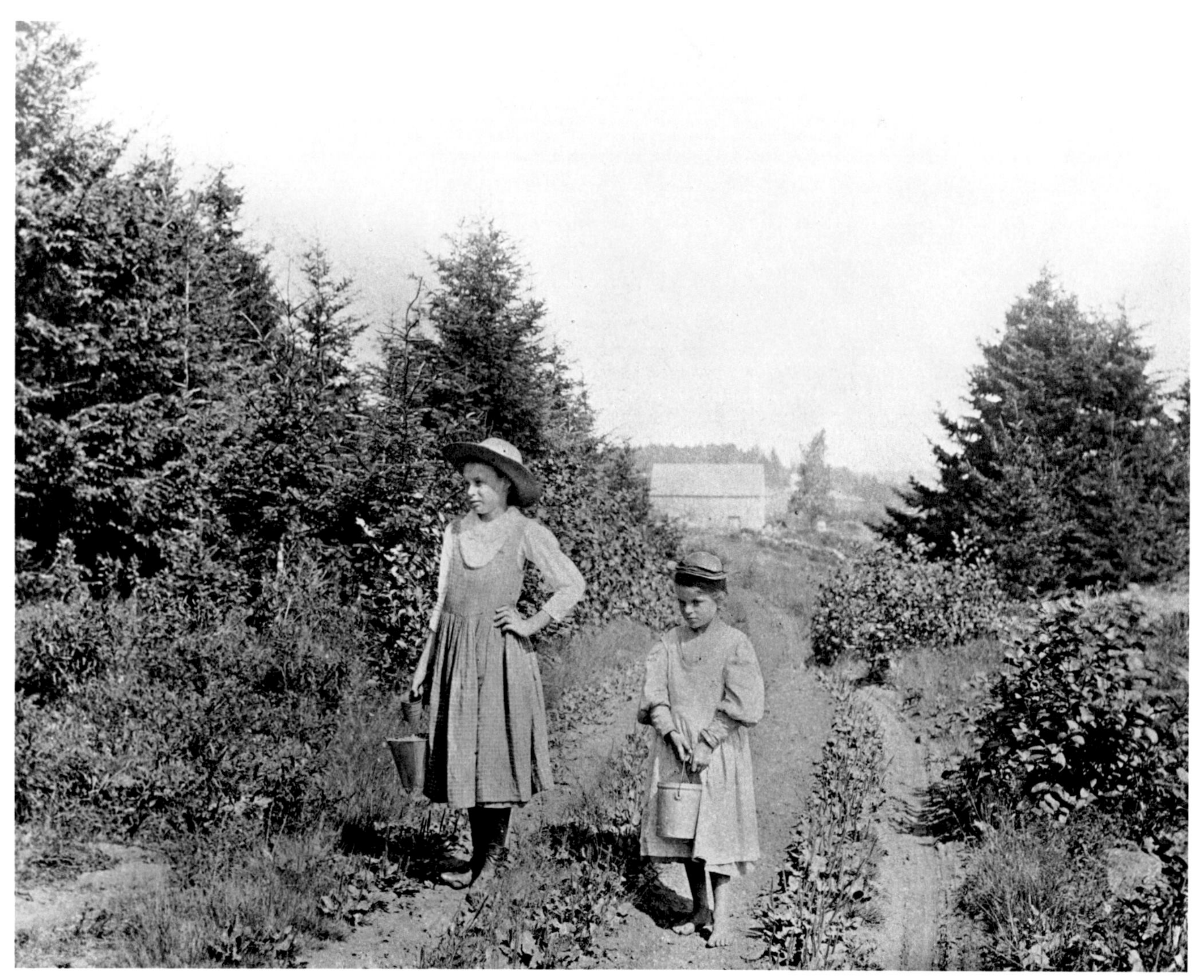

30. Untitled

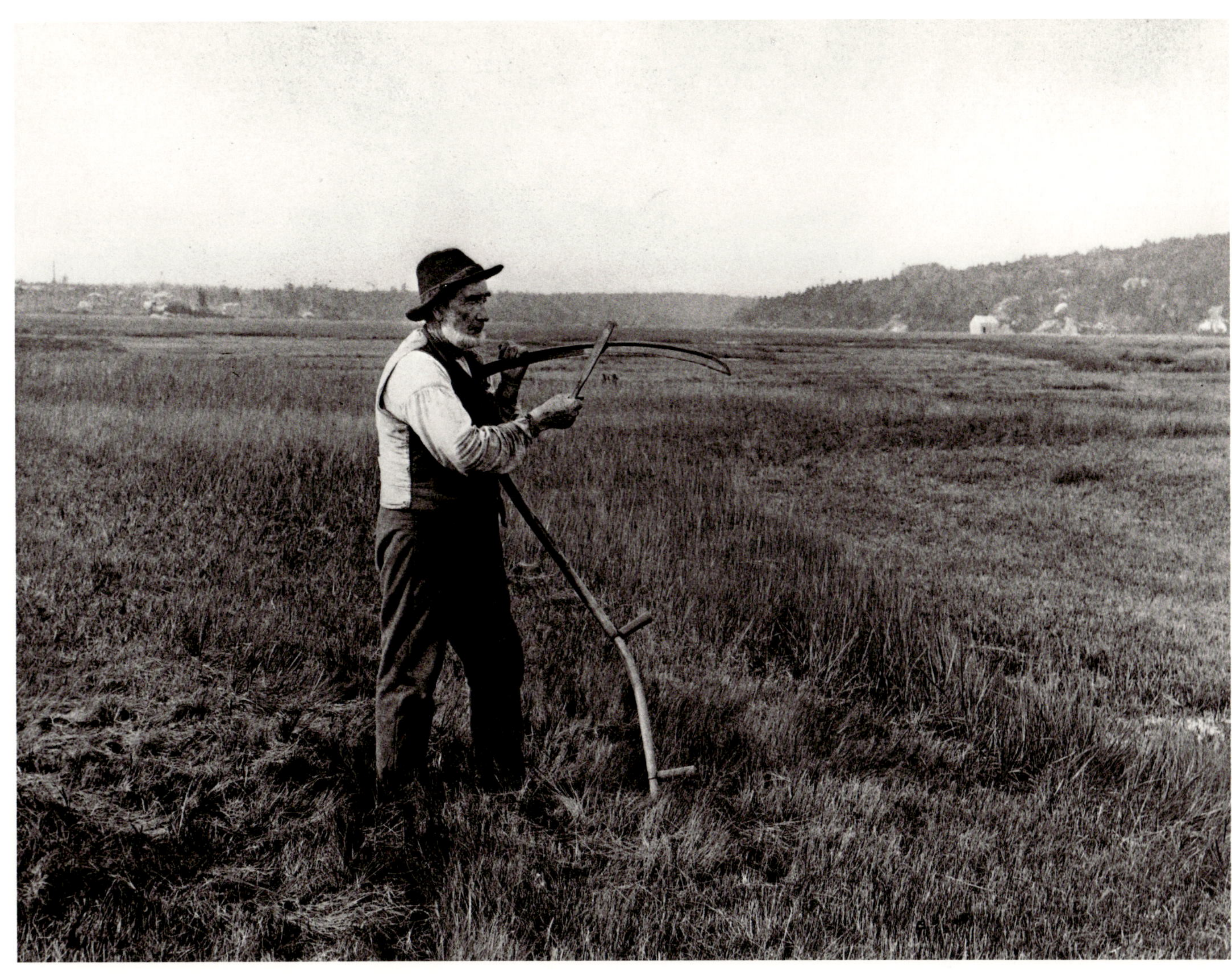

31. Whetting The Scythe

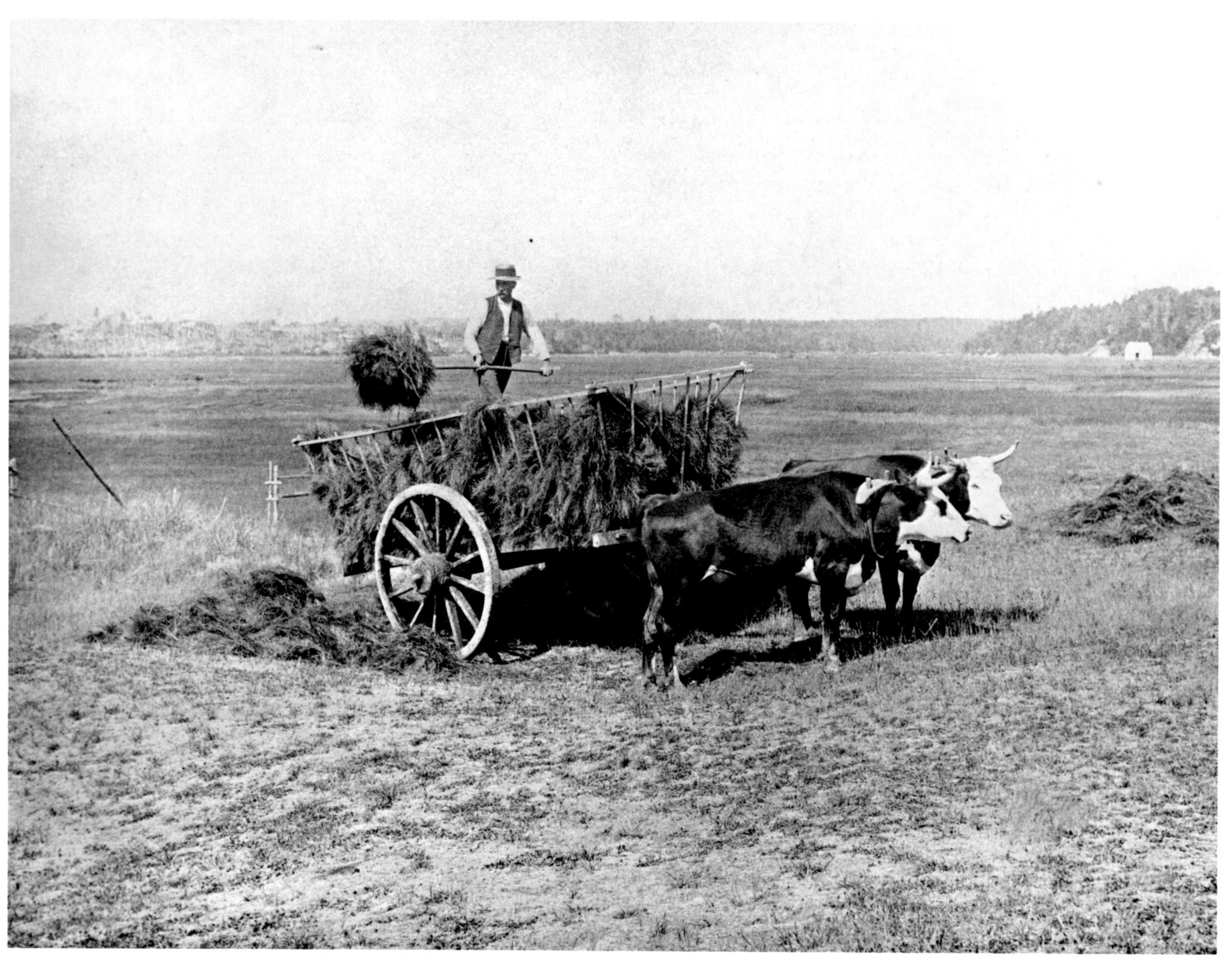

32. Unloading Marsh Hay

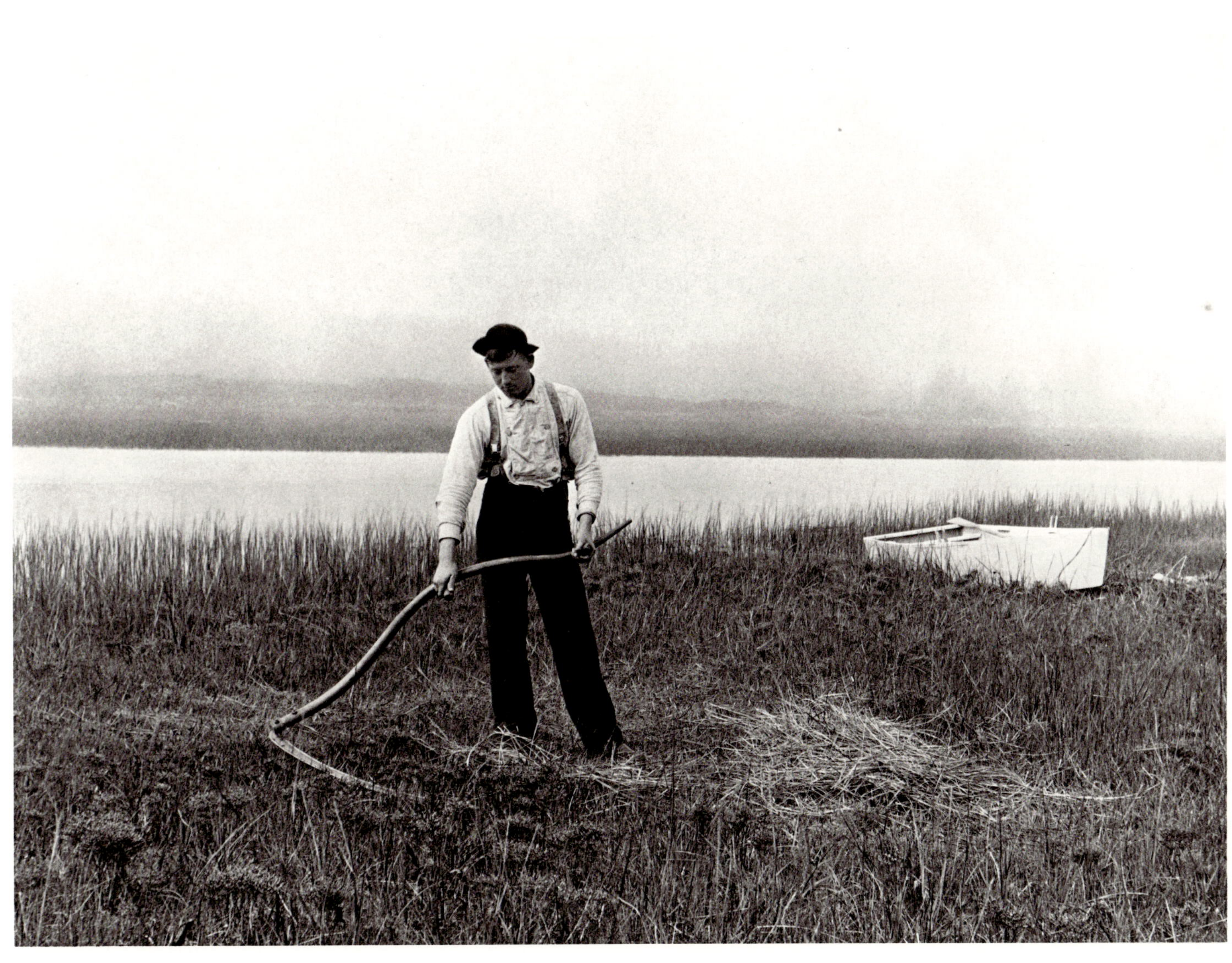

33. Cutting Thatch

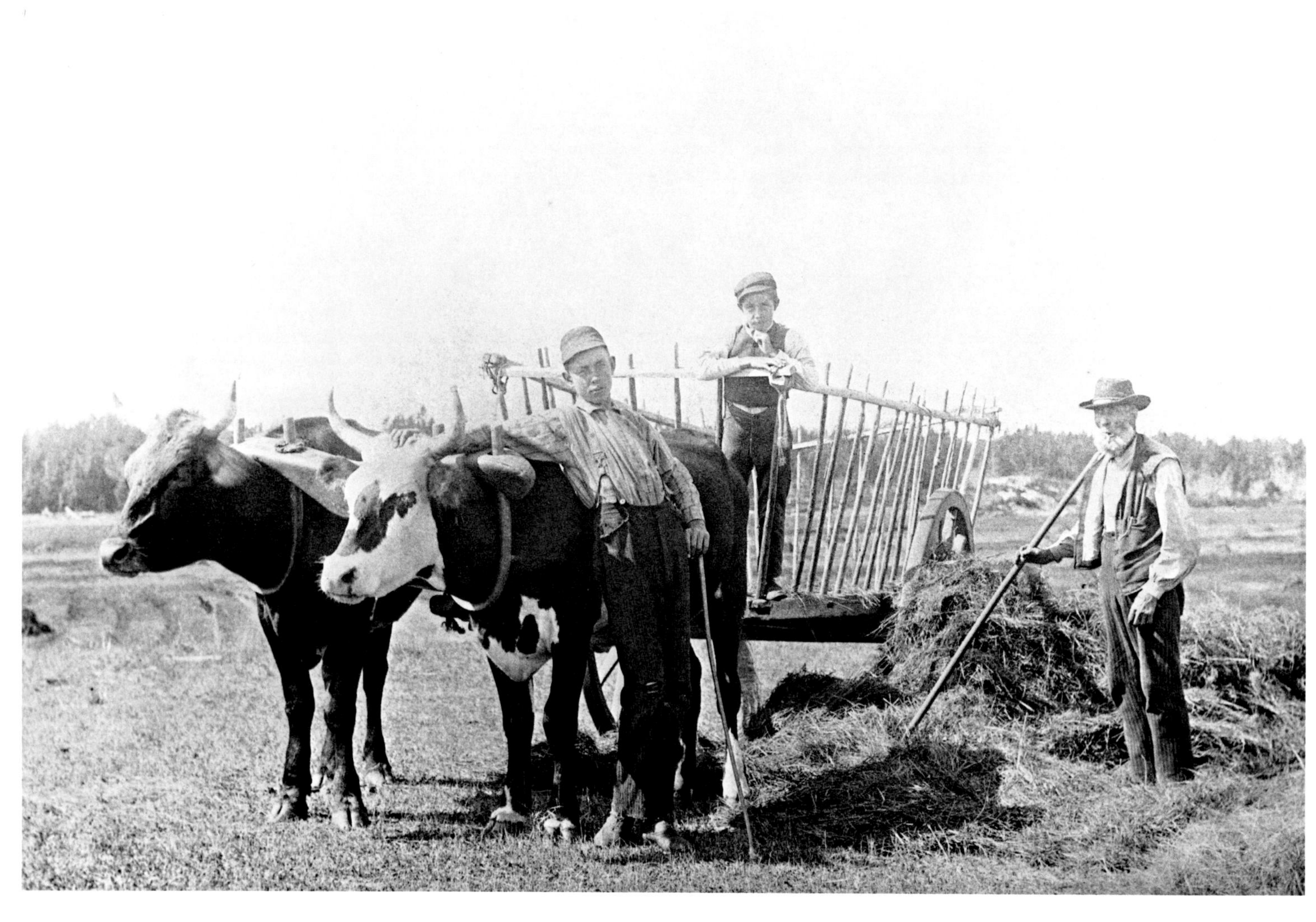

34. *Just Unloaded*

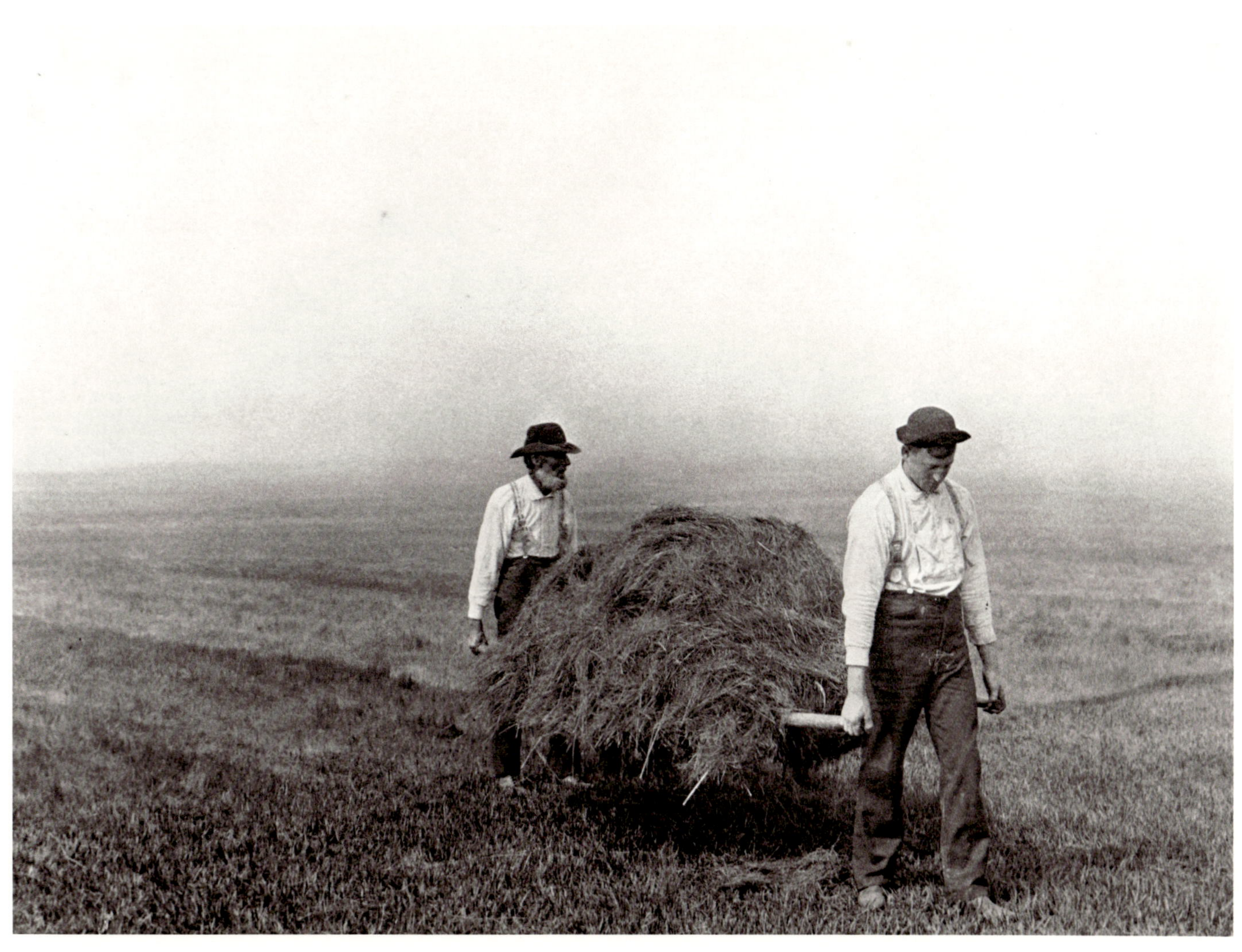

35. *Poling Hay—A Foggy Day On The Marshes*

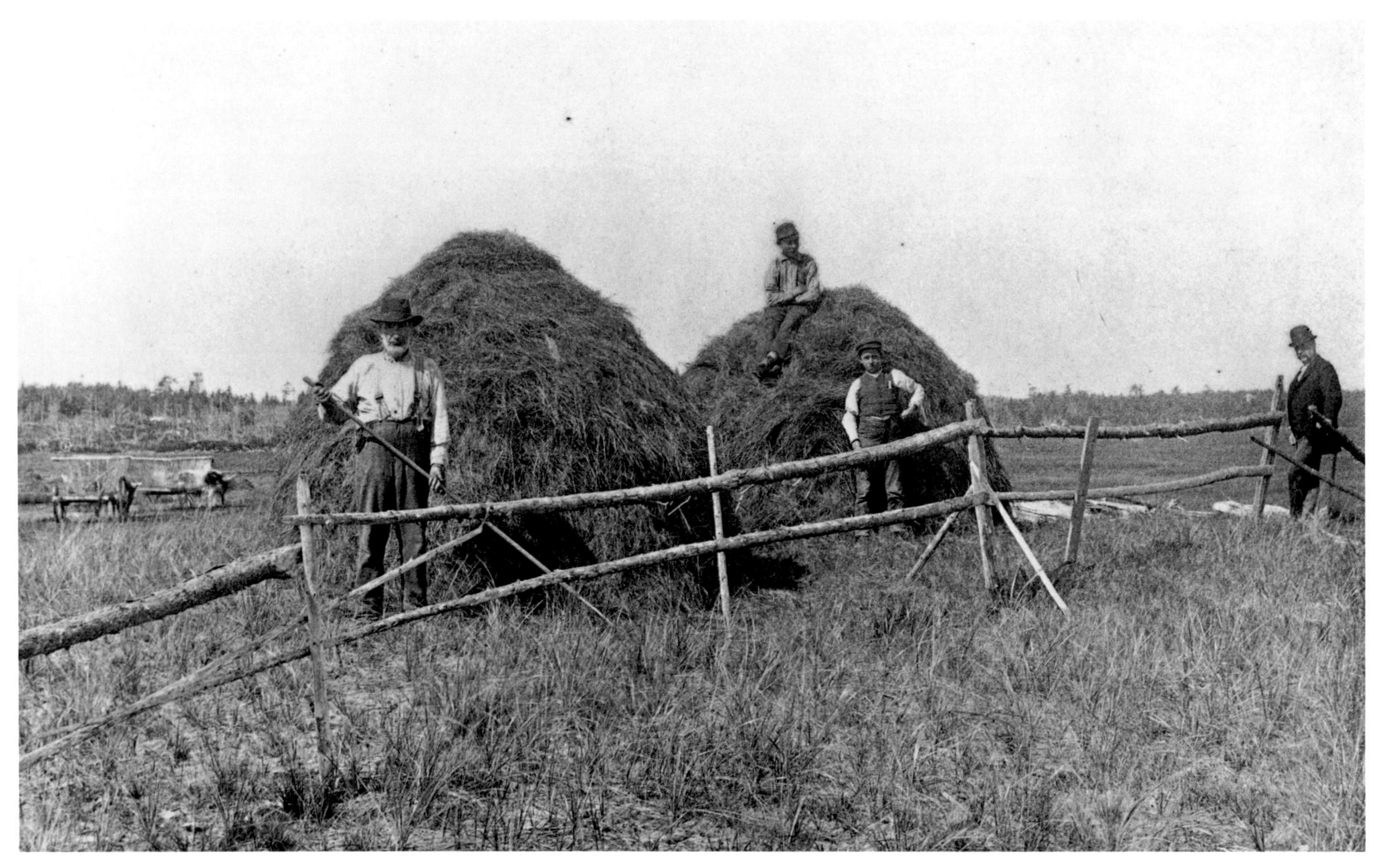

36. Untitled

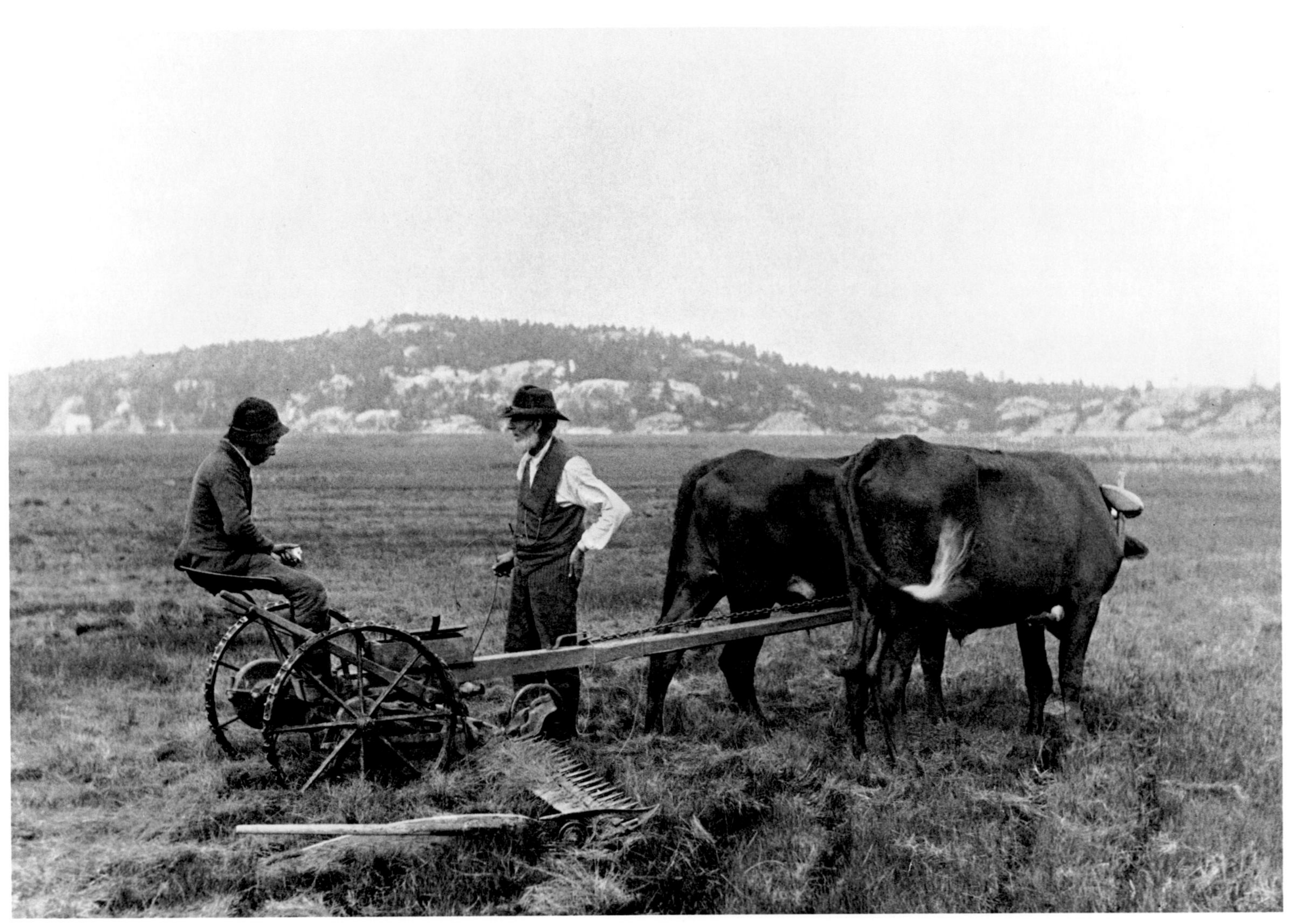

37. The Mowers

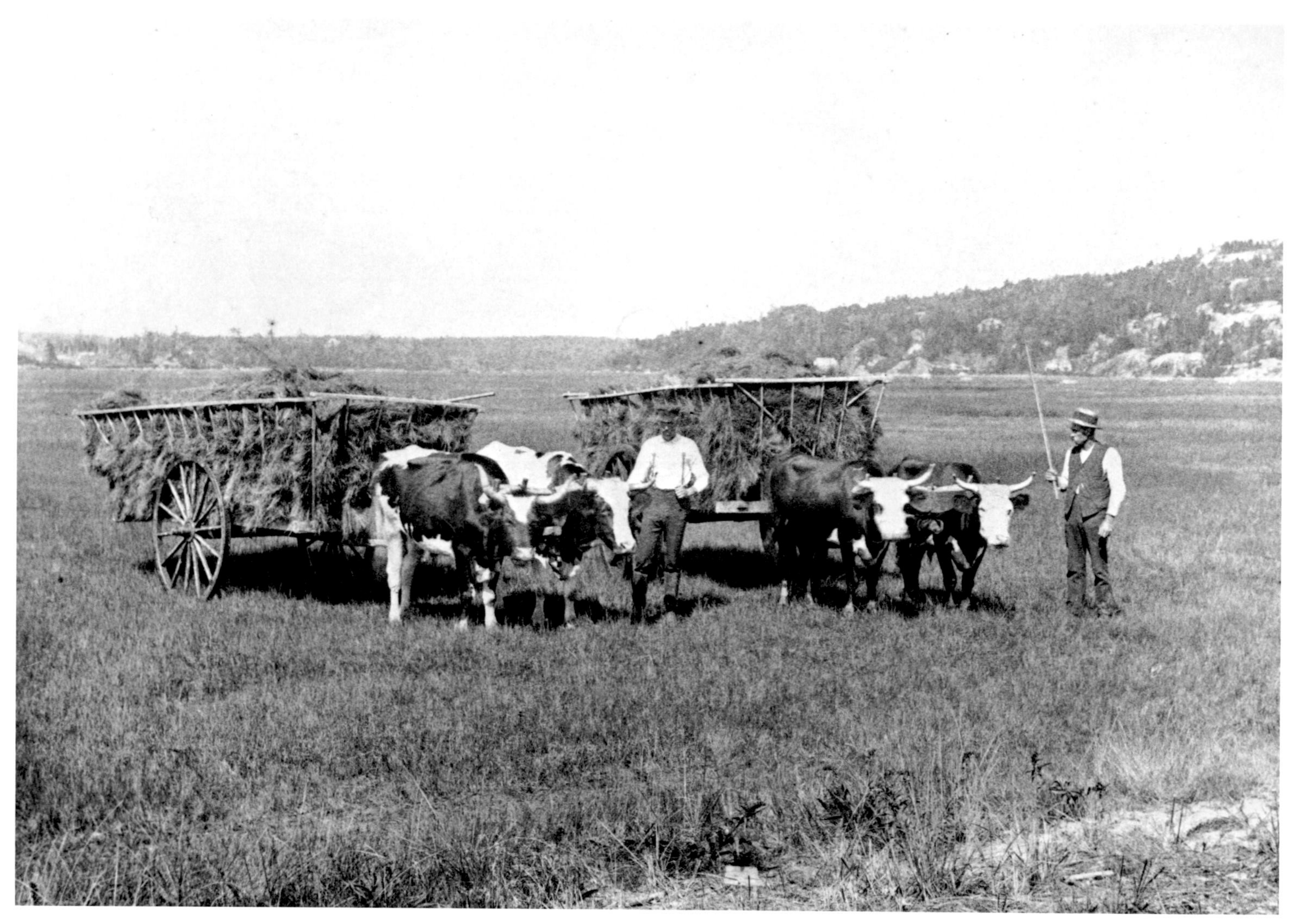

38. On The Marshes

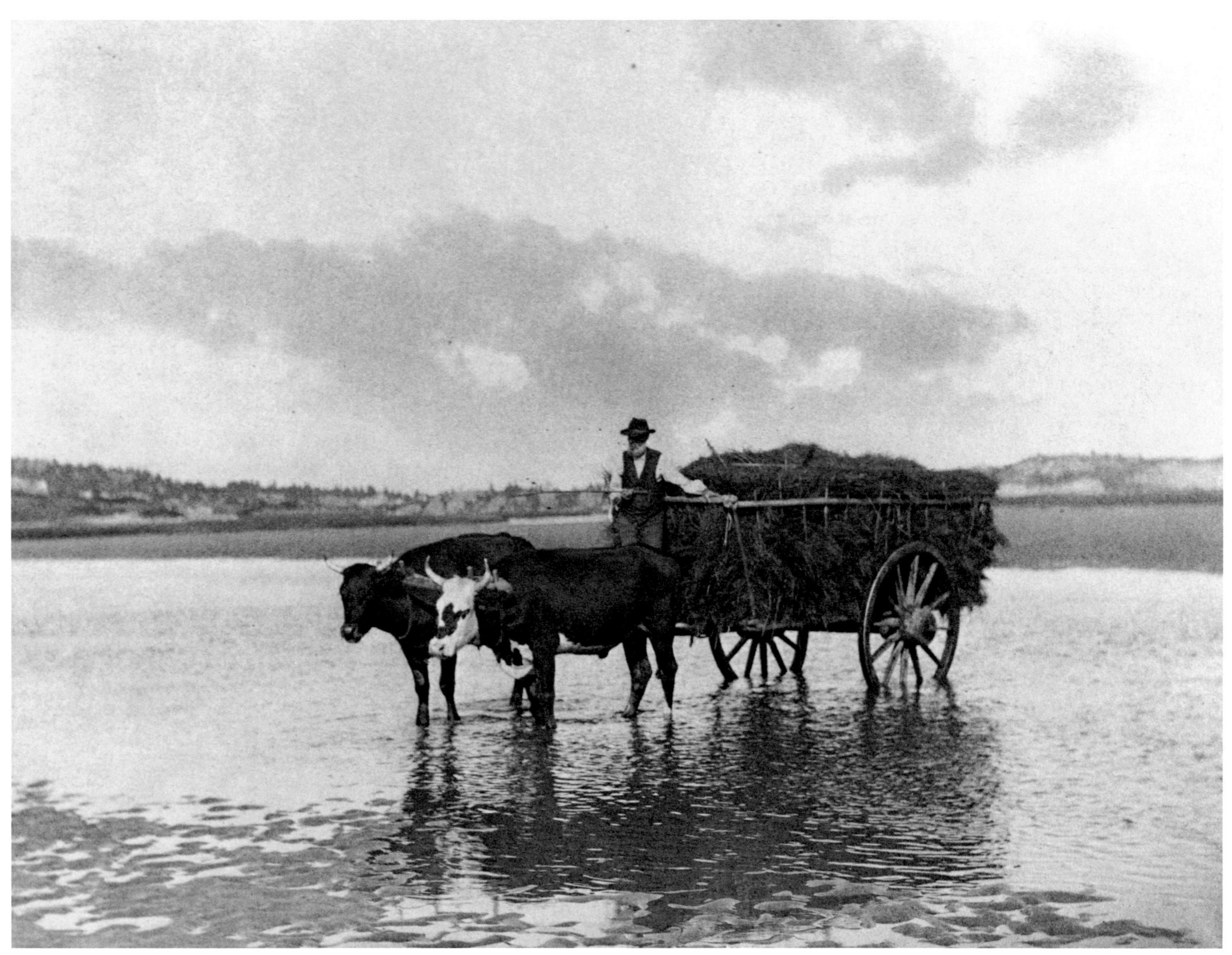

39. Fording The River

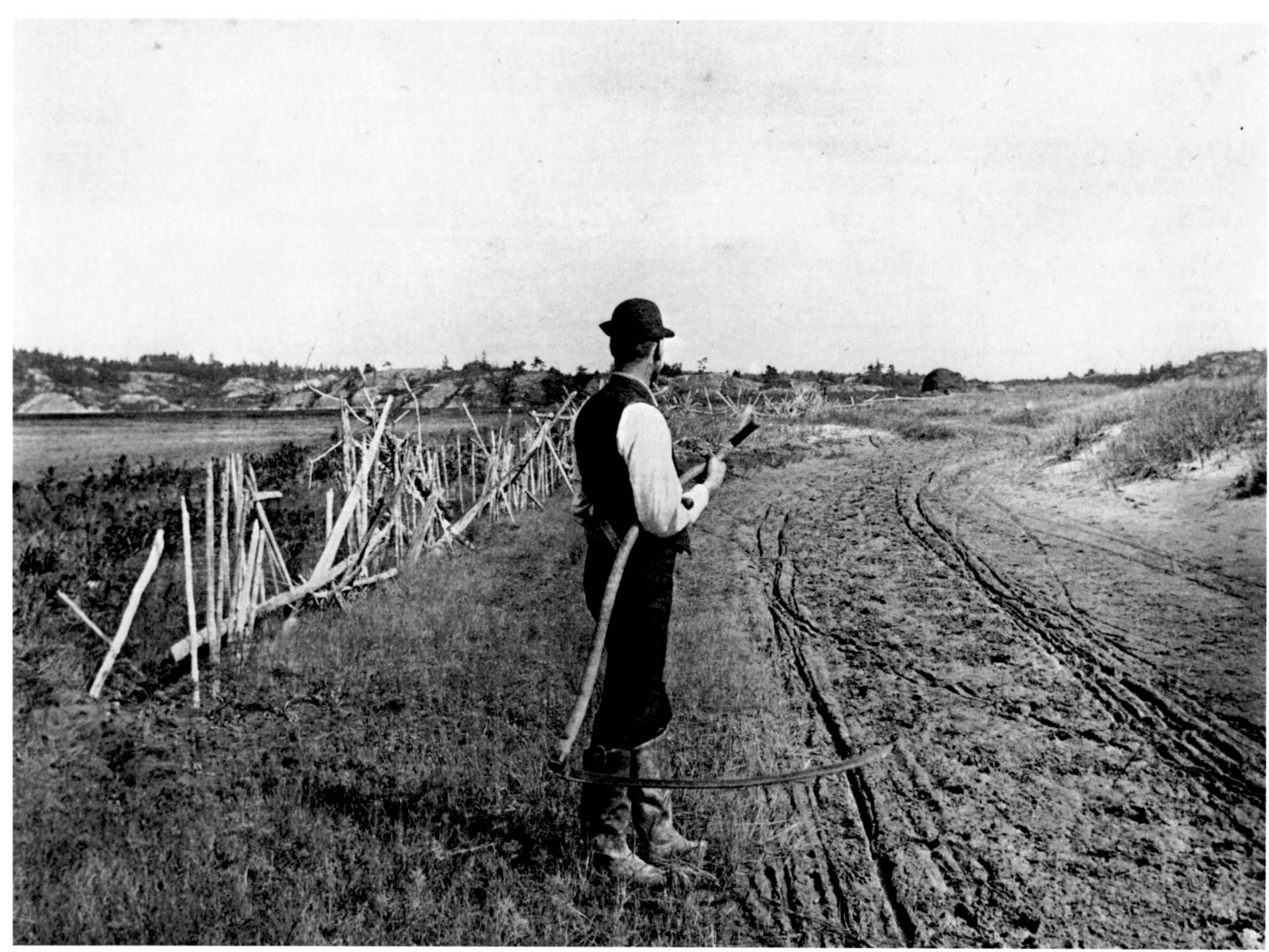

40. *Untitled*

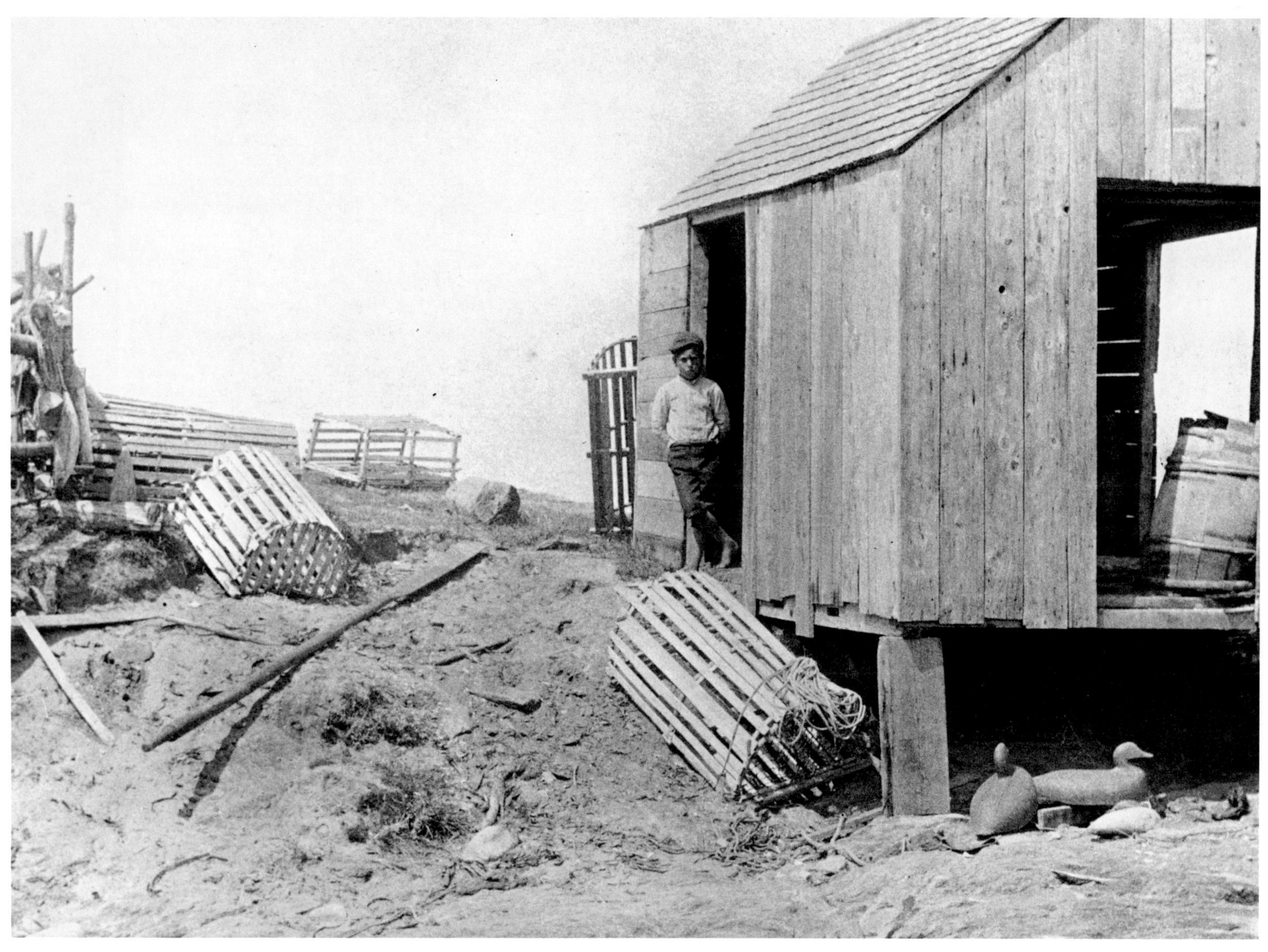

41. *Herbert Wallace In His Father's Fish House*

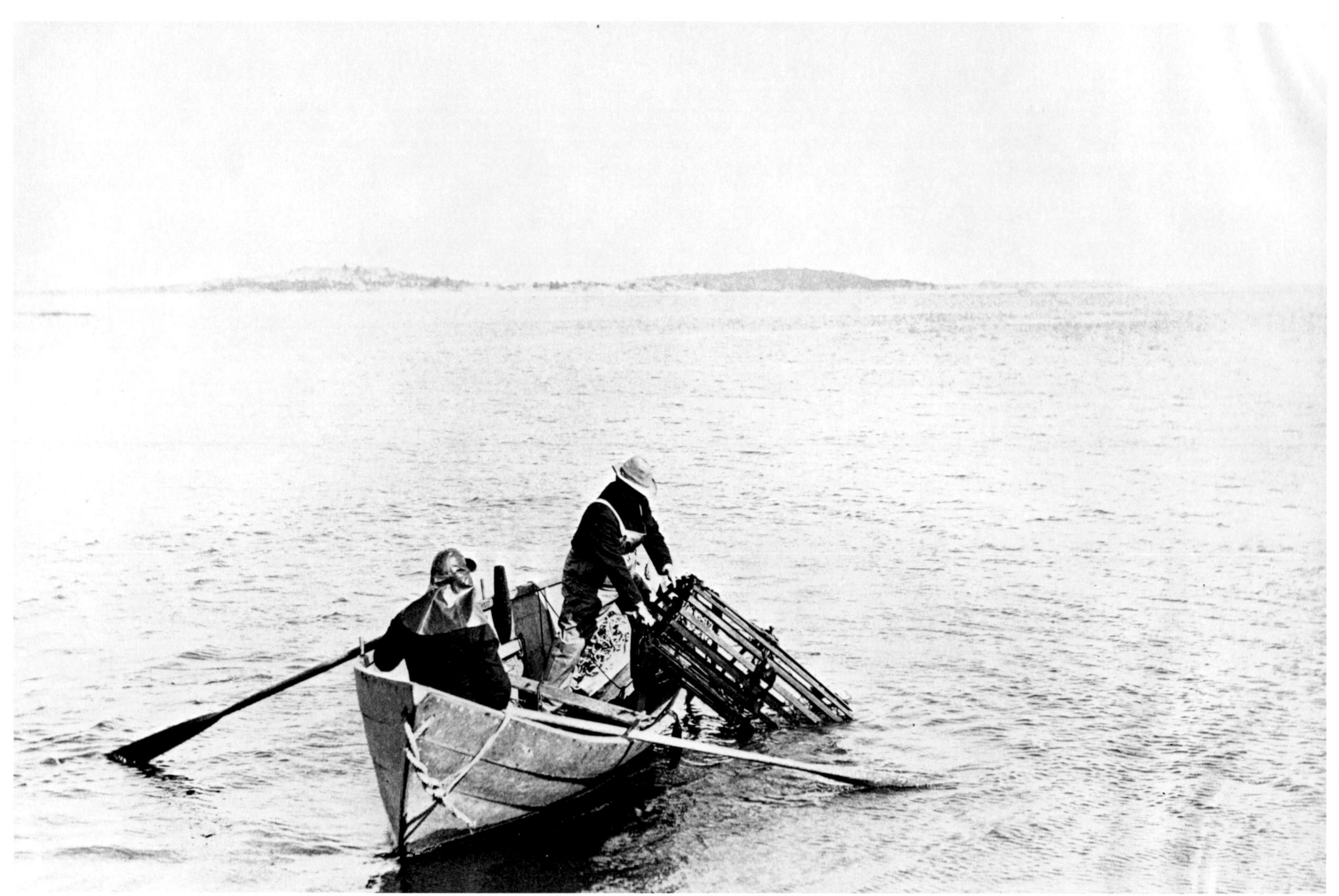

42. Pulling Traps

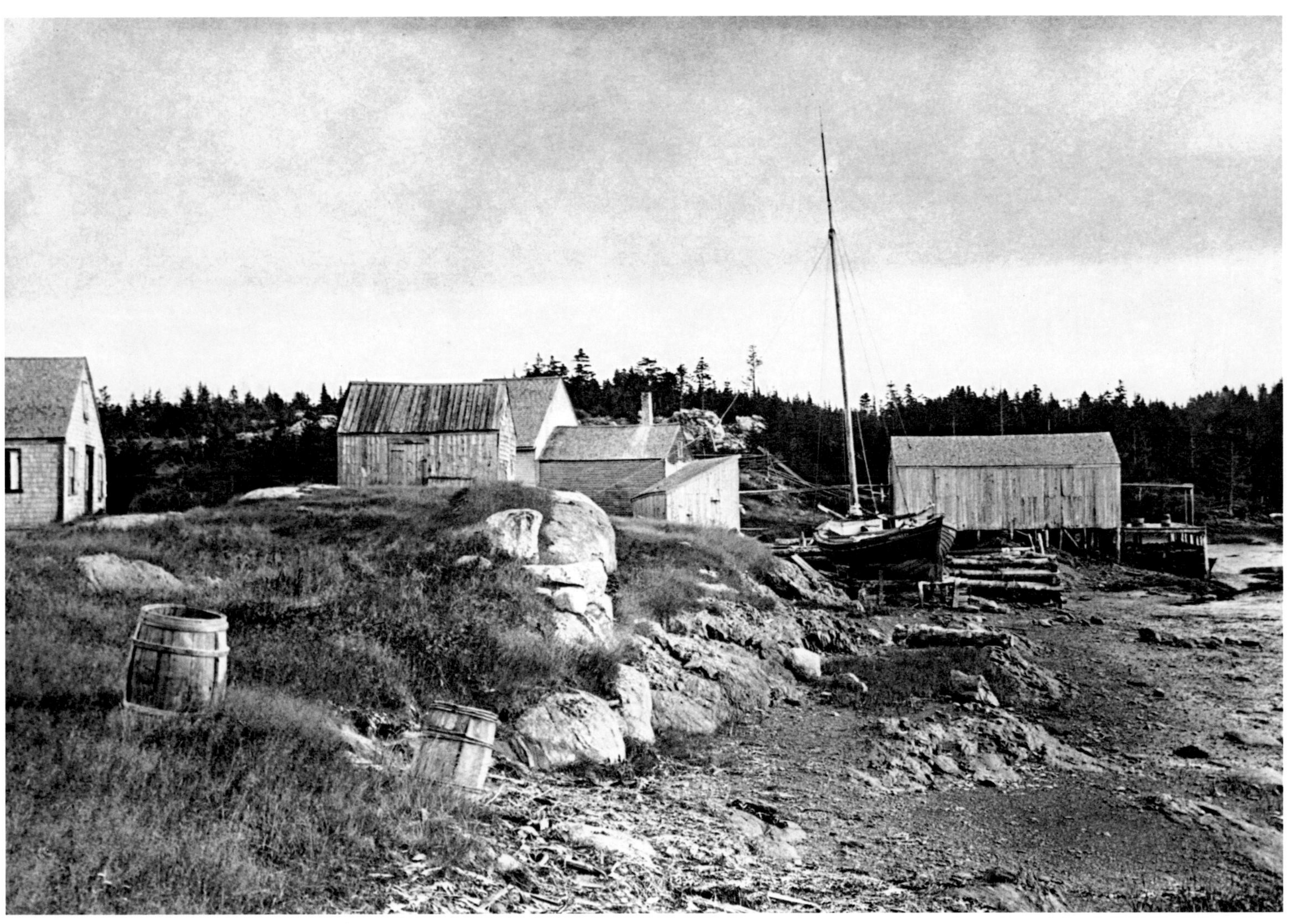

43. *Alliquippa Harbor—Small Point*

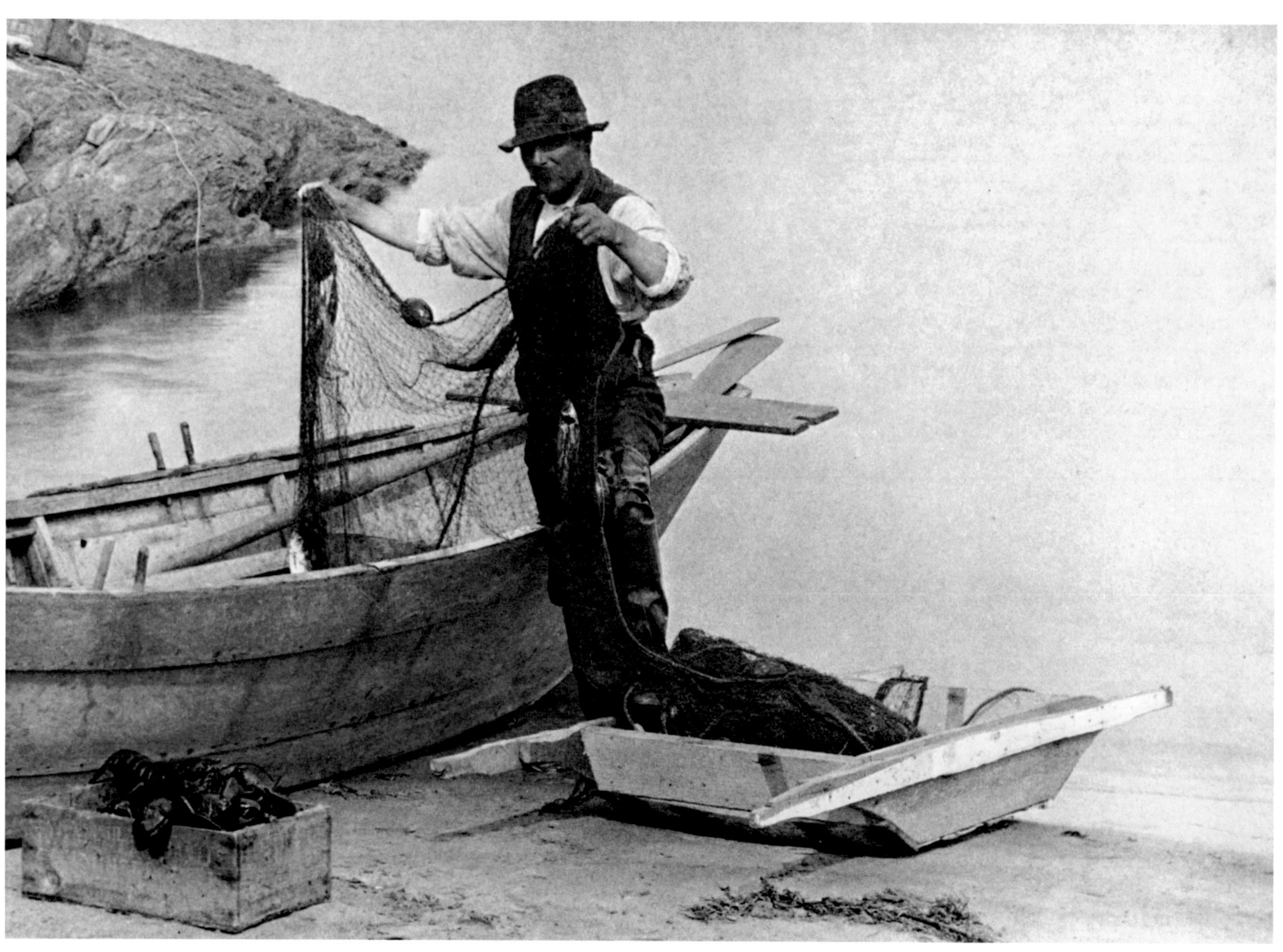

44. Small Point

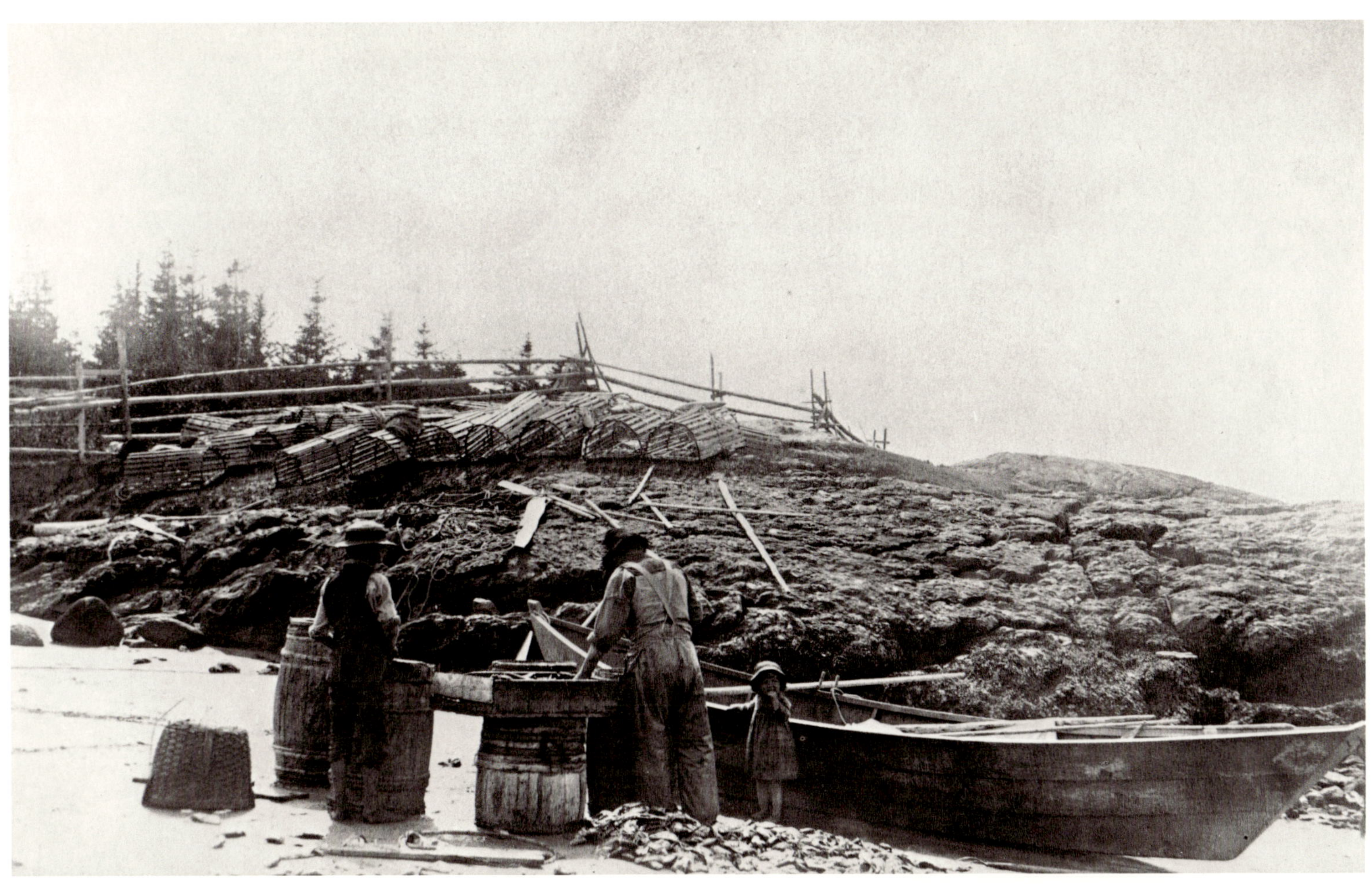

45. *Salting Bait—Small Point 1888*

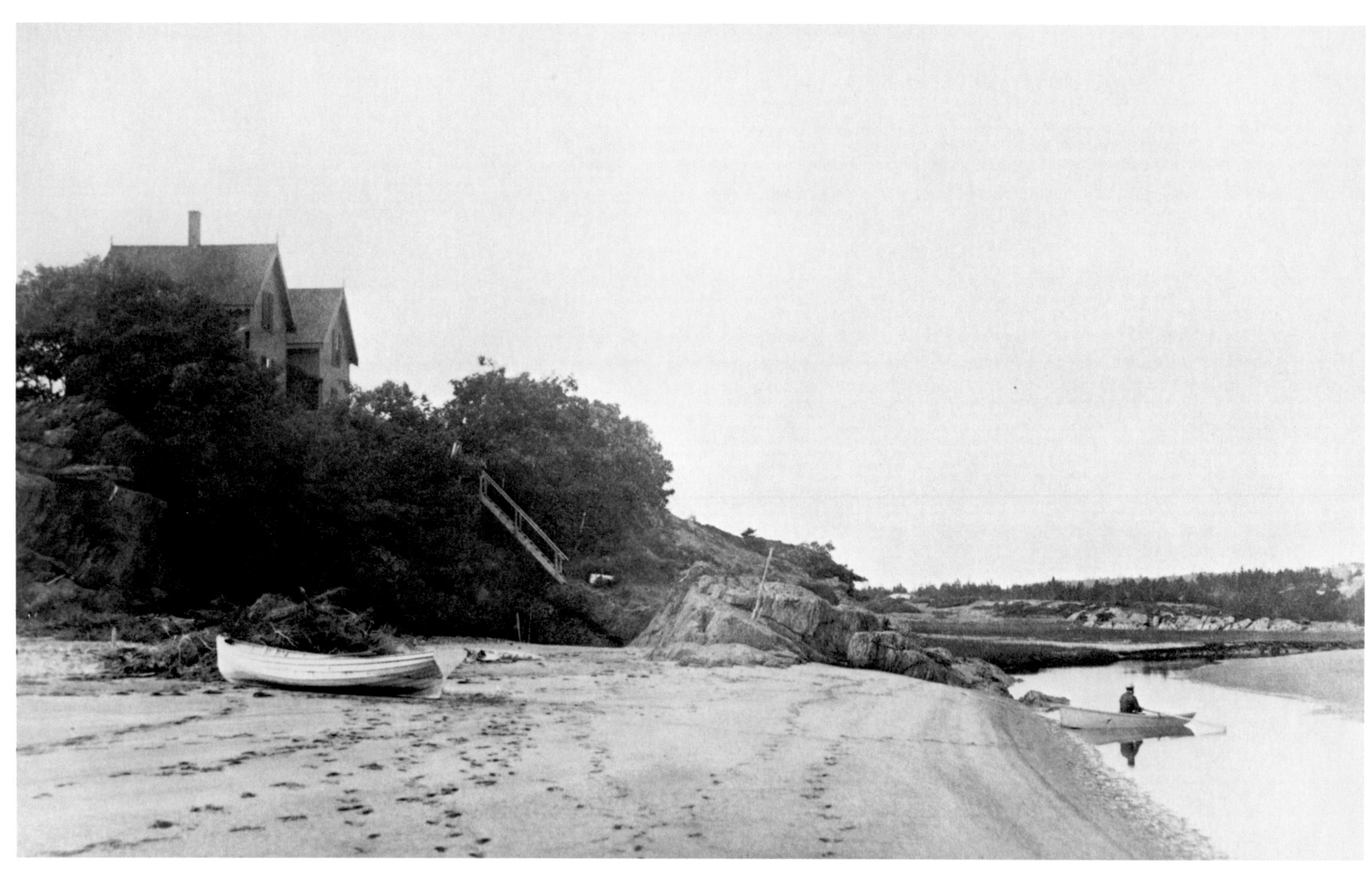

46. Anderson Cottage—Small Point 1888

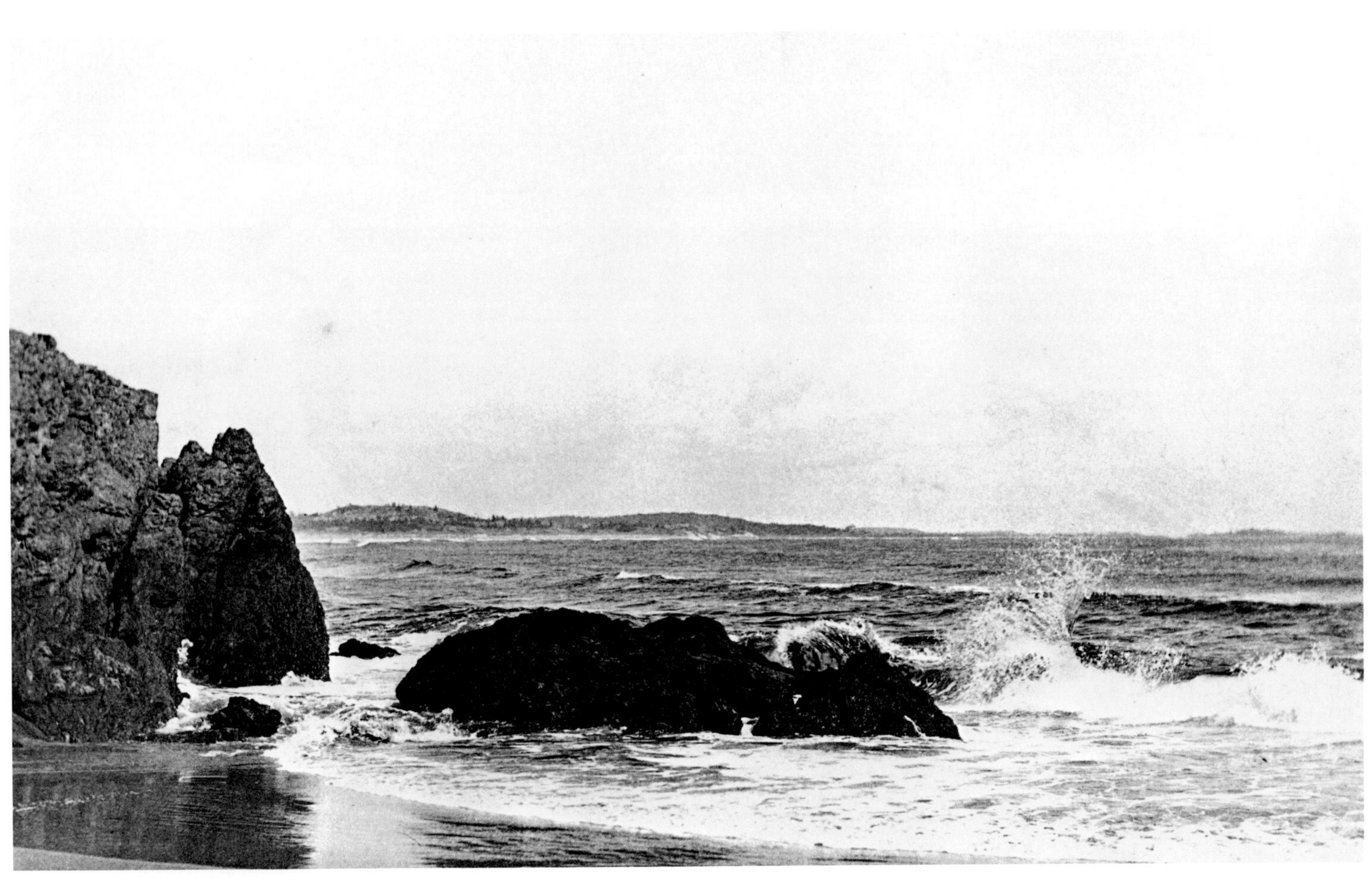

47. *End Of The Bluff—Small Point*

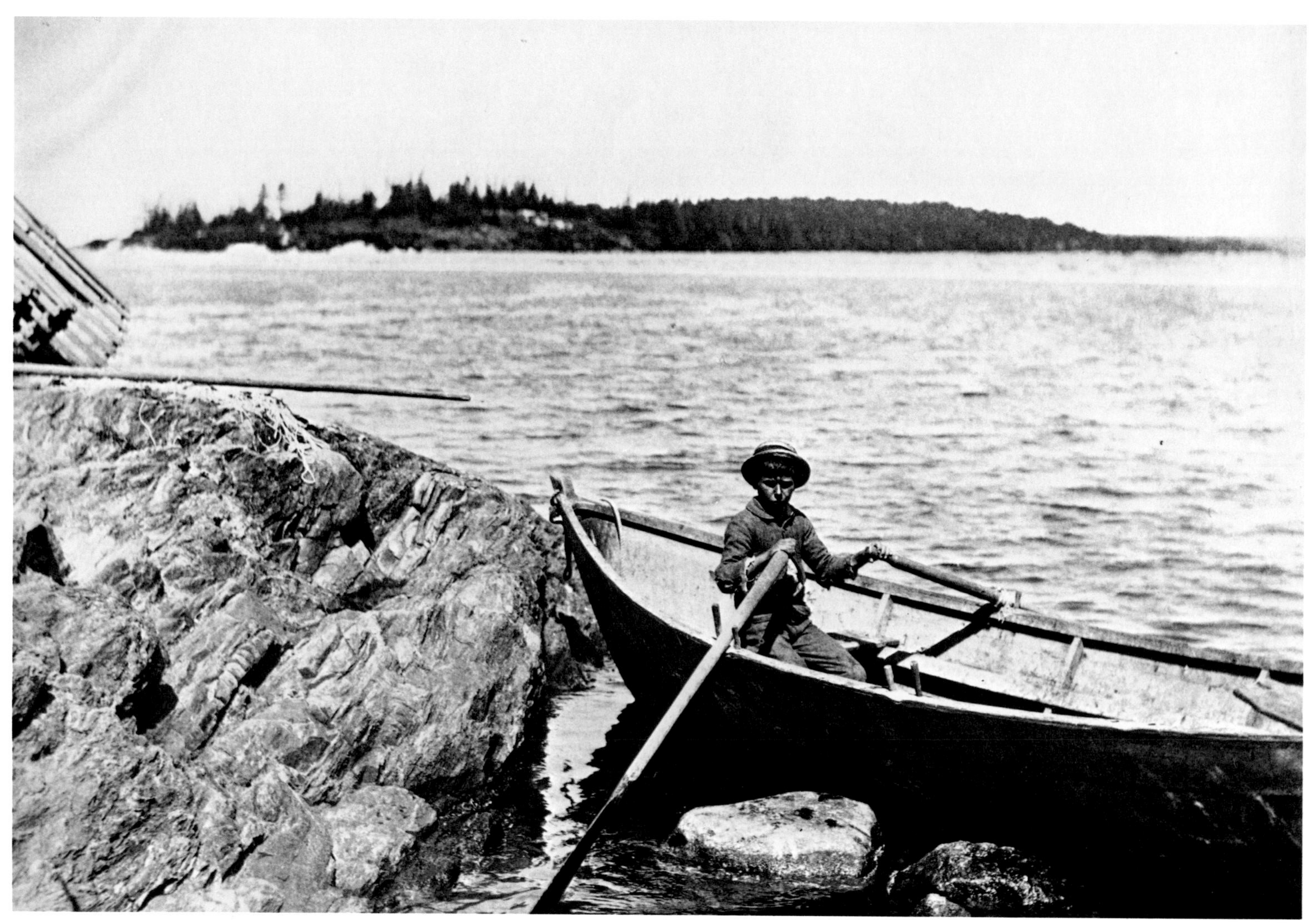

48. The Young Boatman

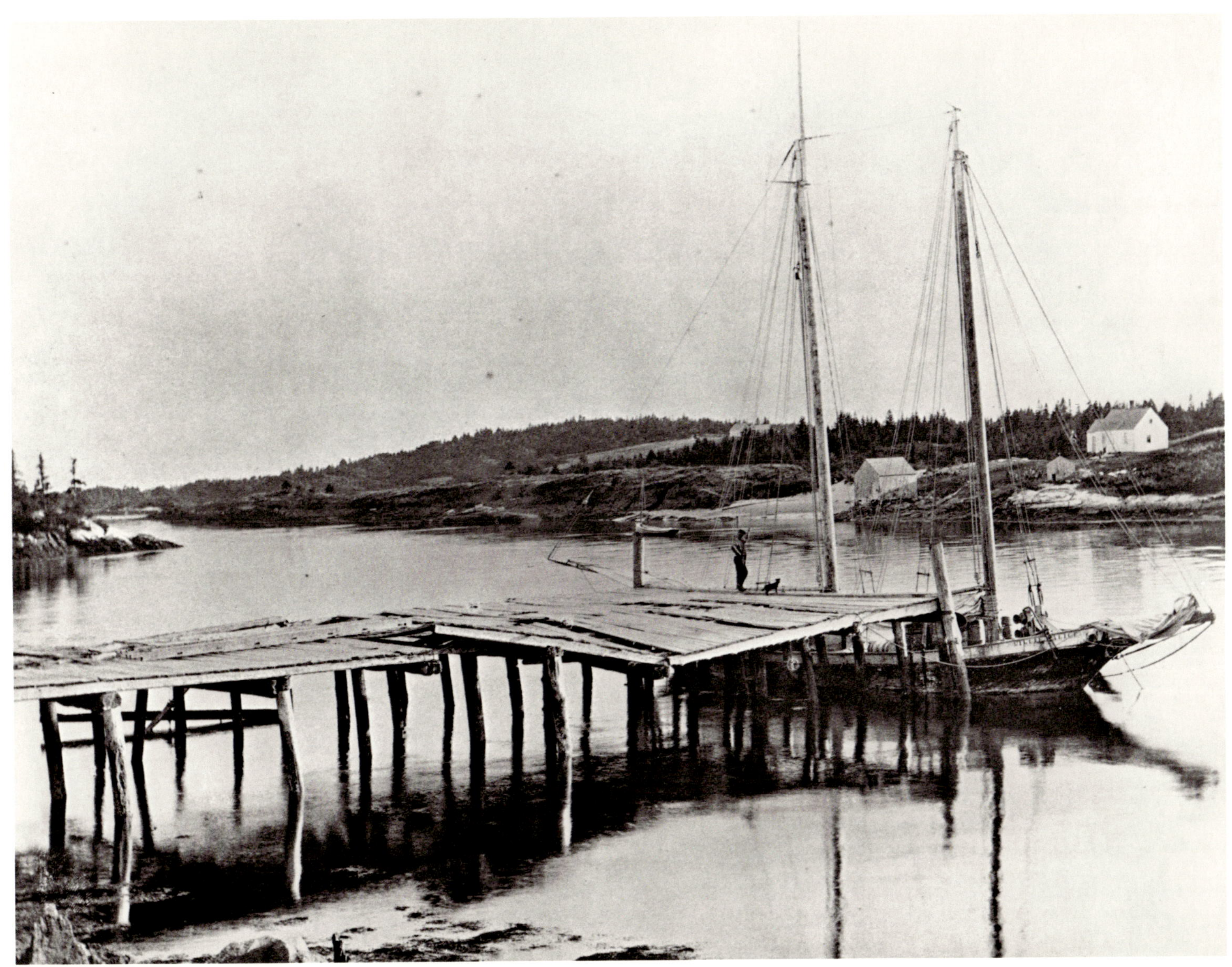

49. *In Alliquippa Harbor*

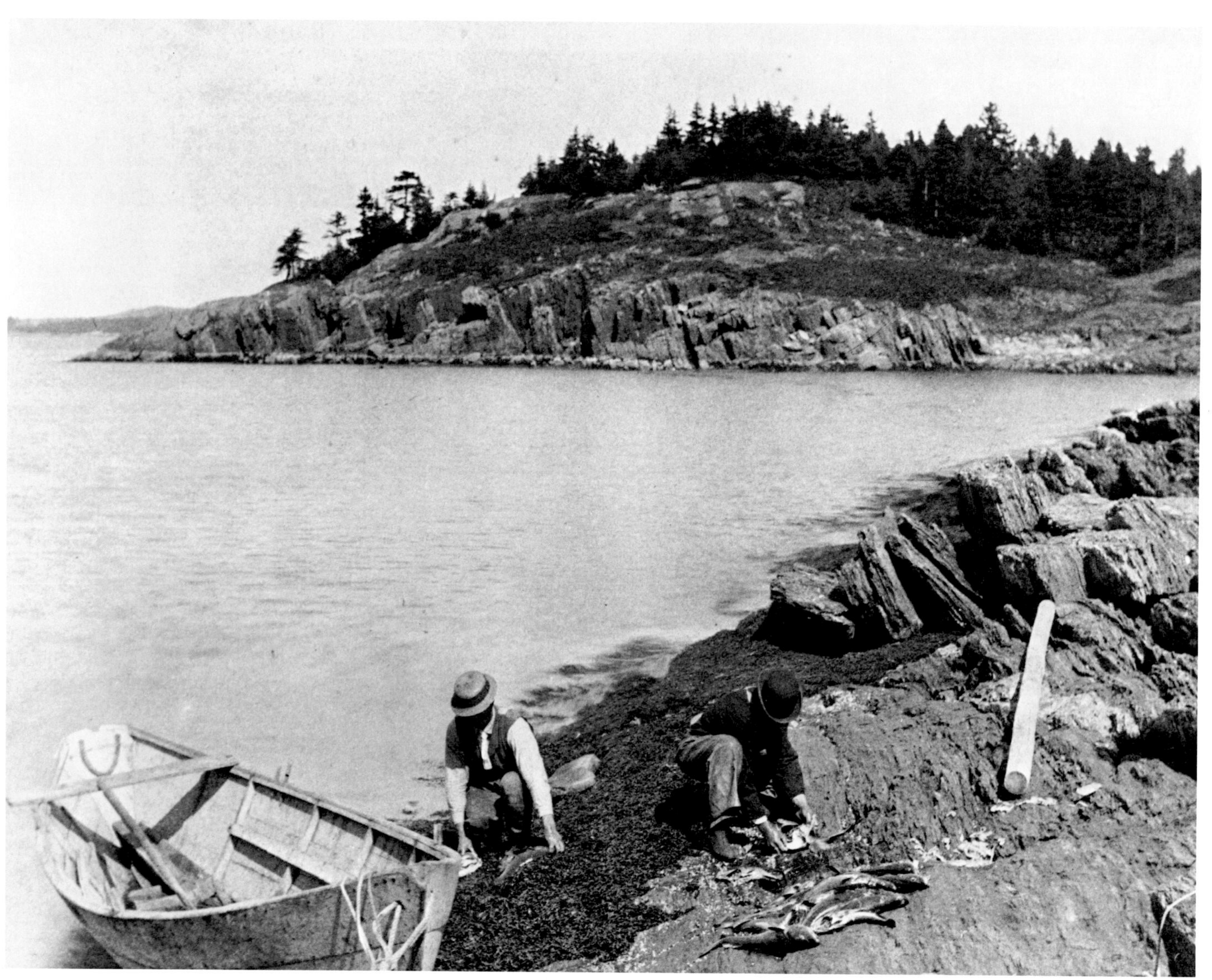

50. *Cleaning Fish*

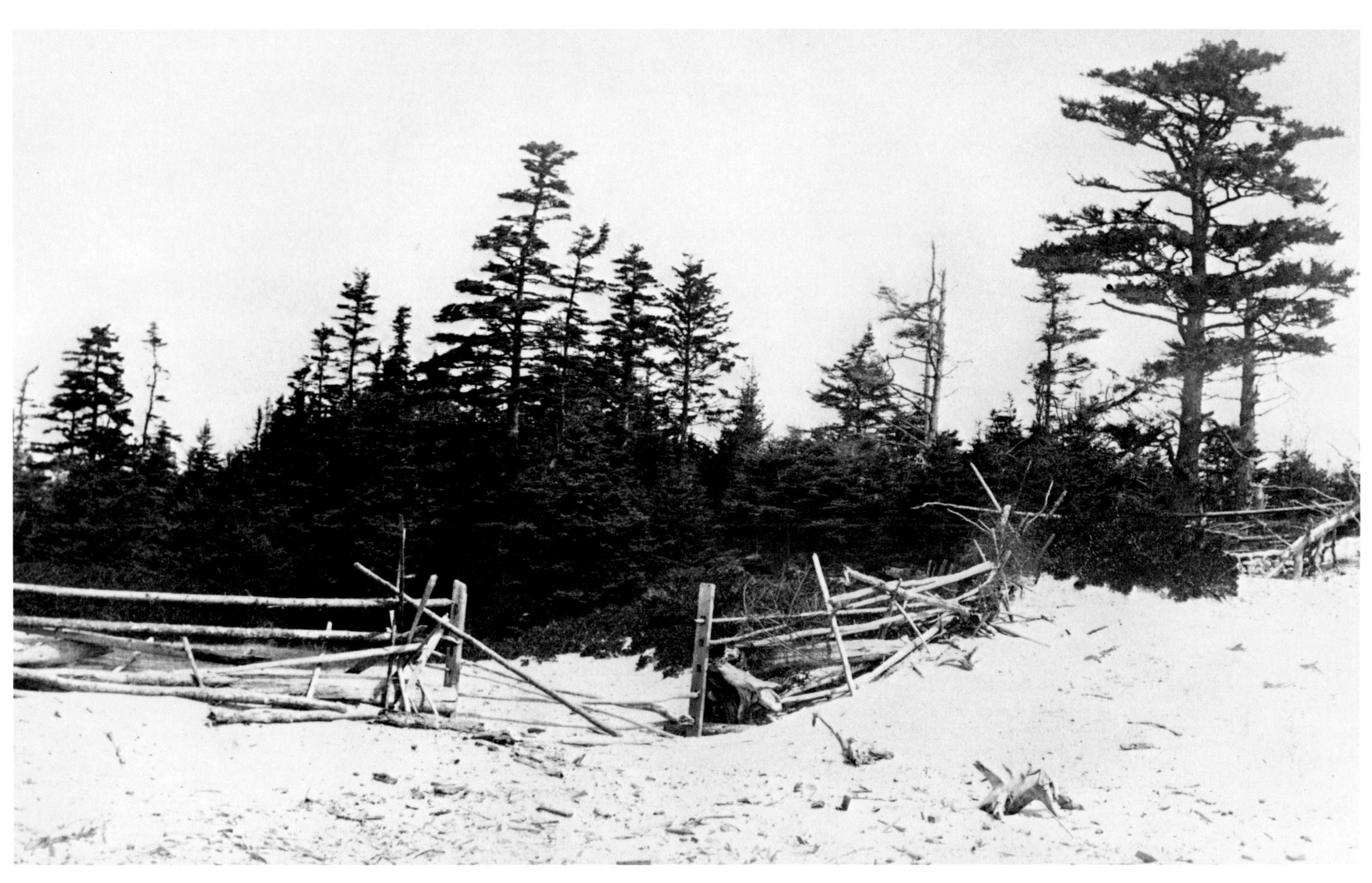

51. Road To Johnson's Pound—Small Point 1889

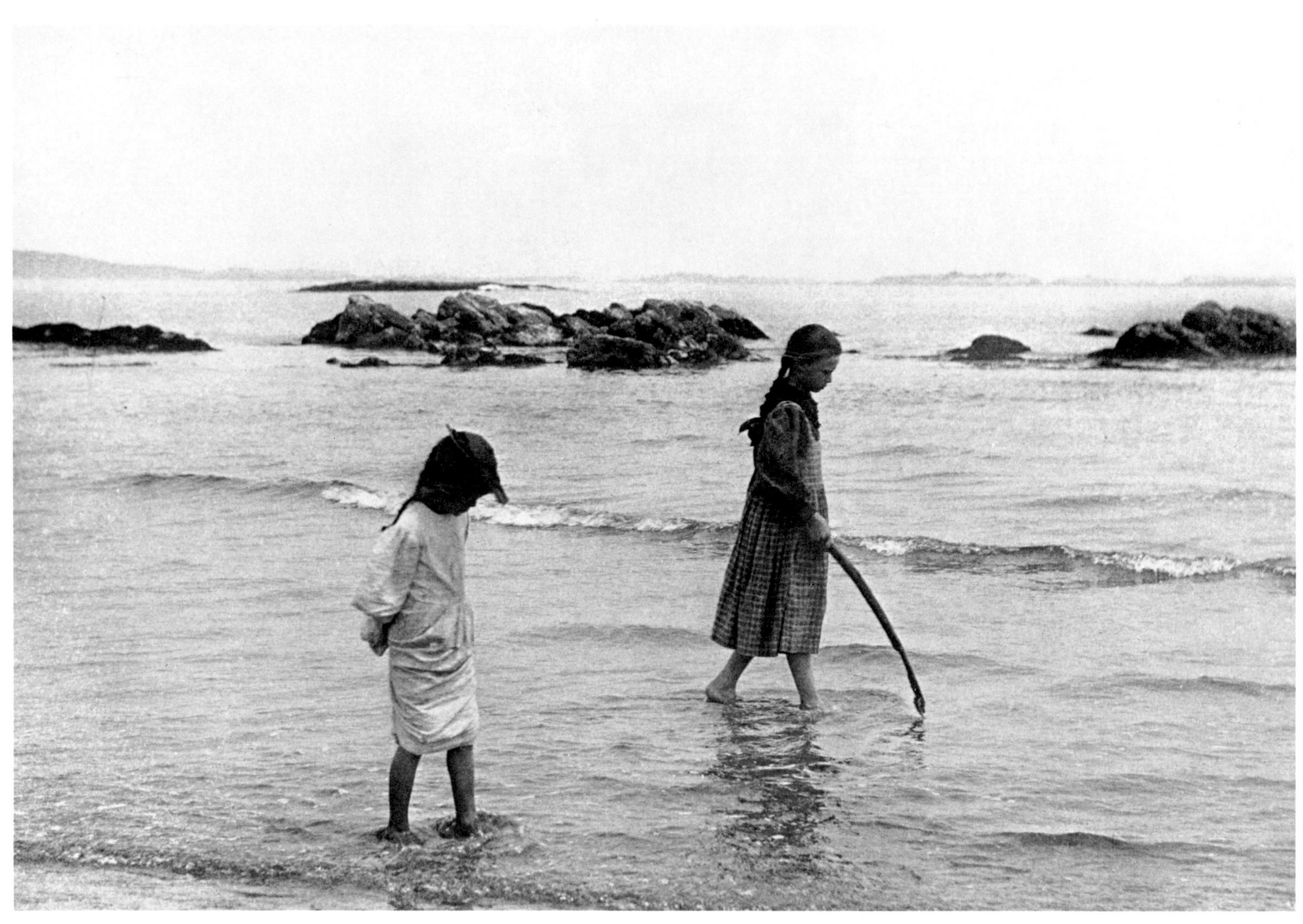

52. *Playing In The Water*

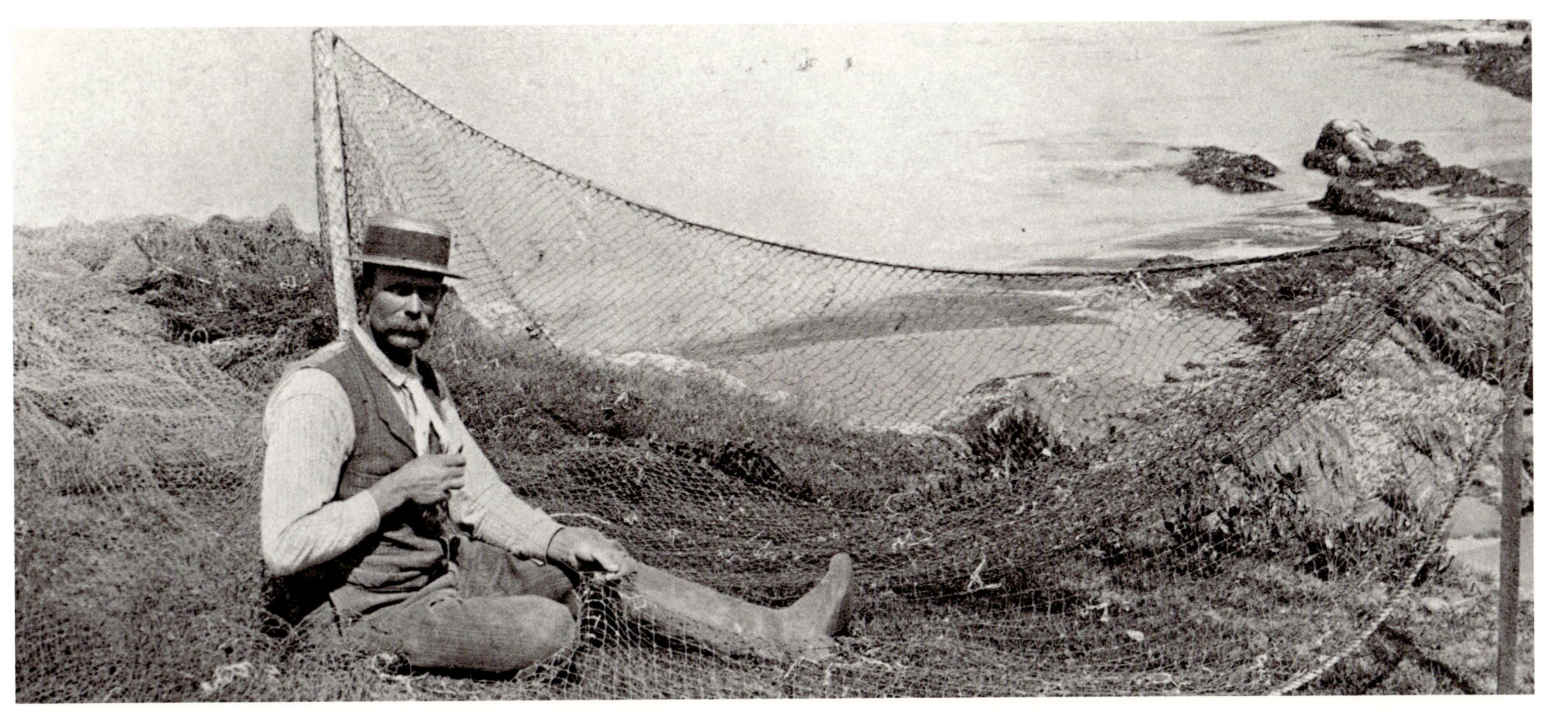

53. Mending The Net

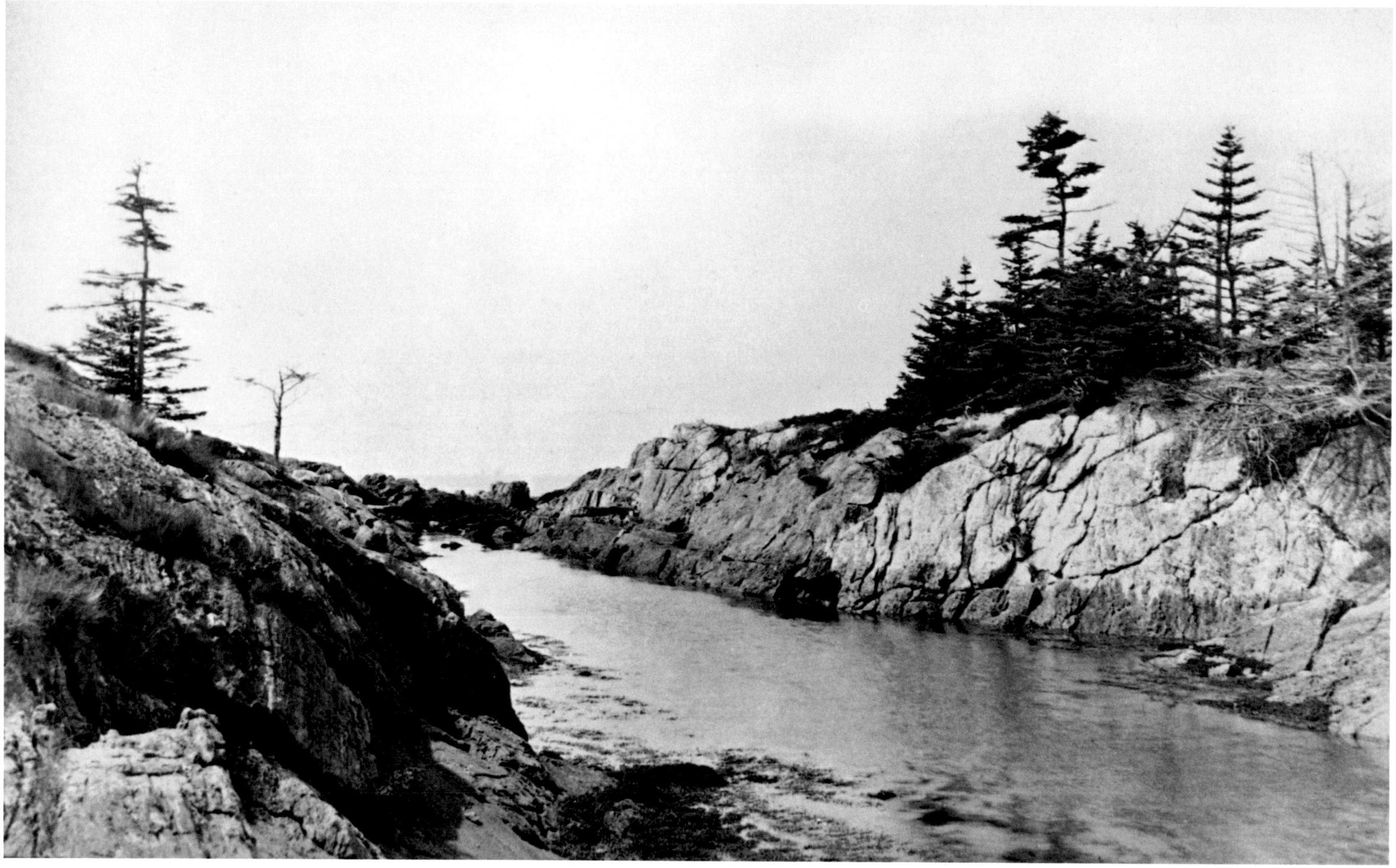

54. Rocky Inlet—Small Point, West Side, 1889

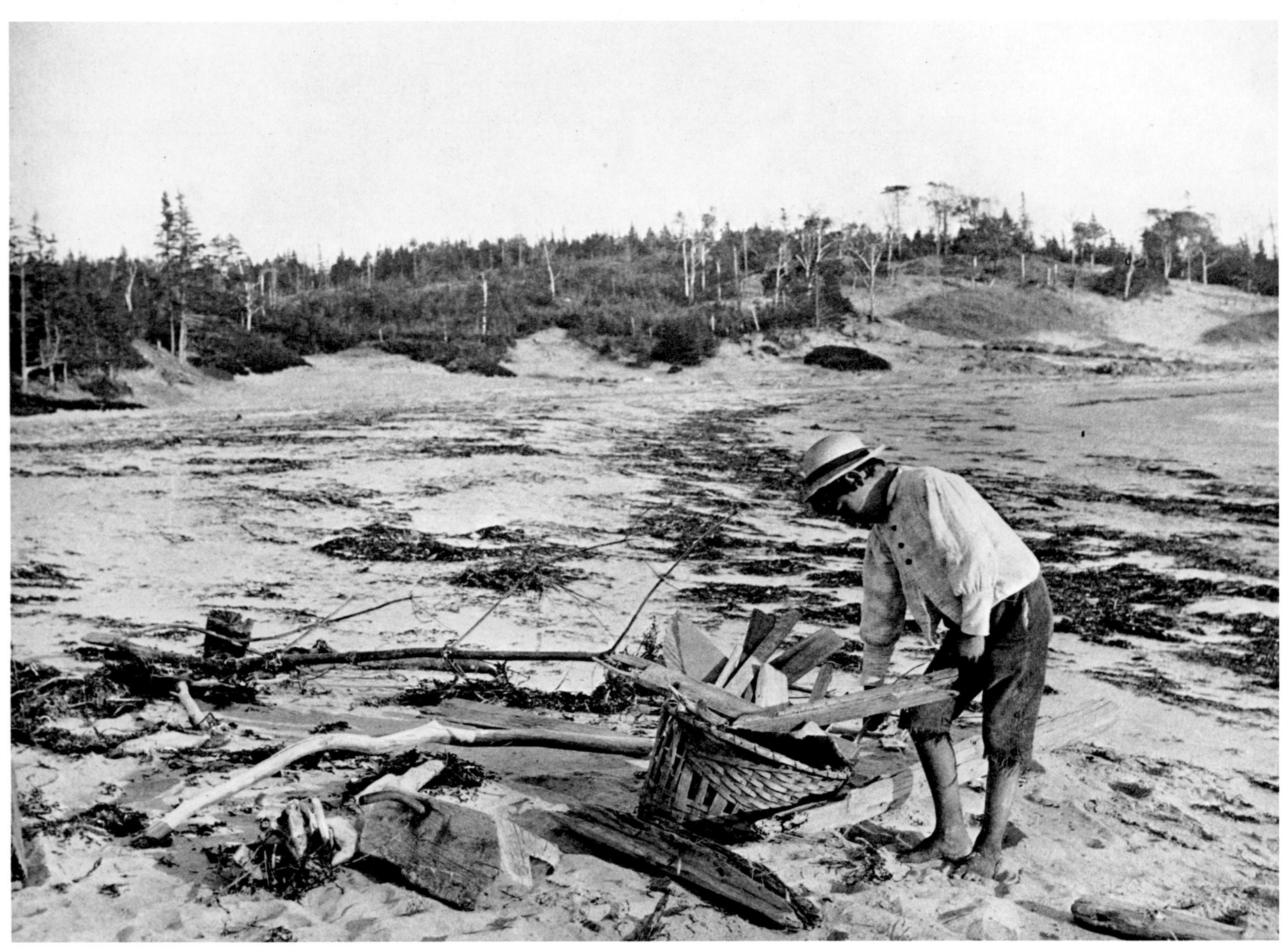

55. *Gathering Driftwood—Head Beach, Small Point*

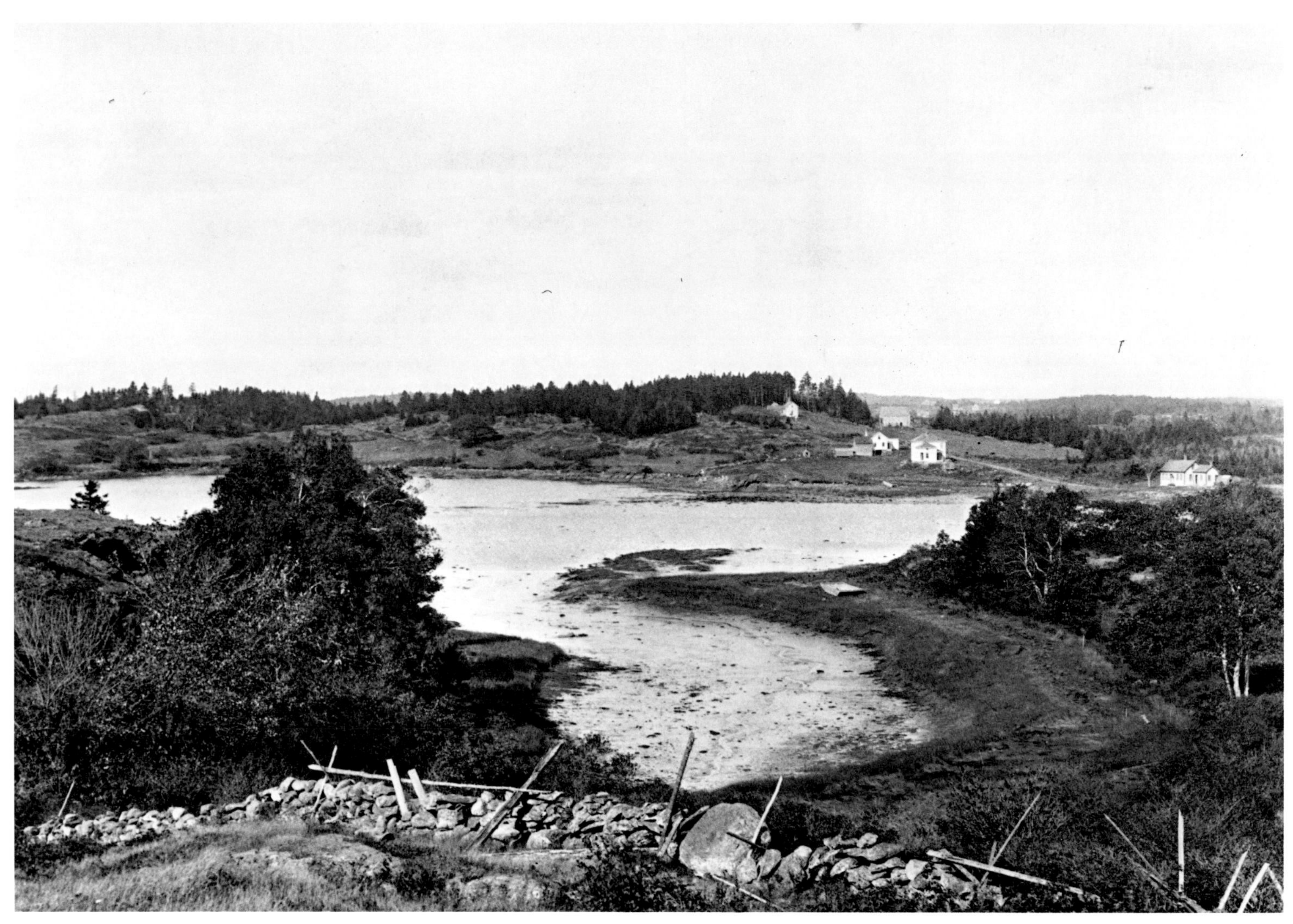

56. *Untitled*

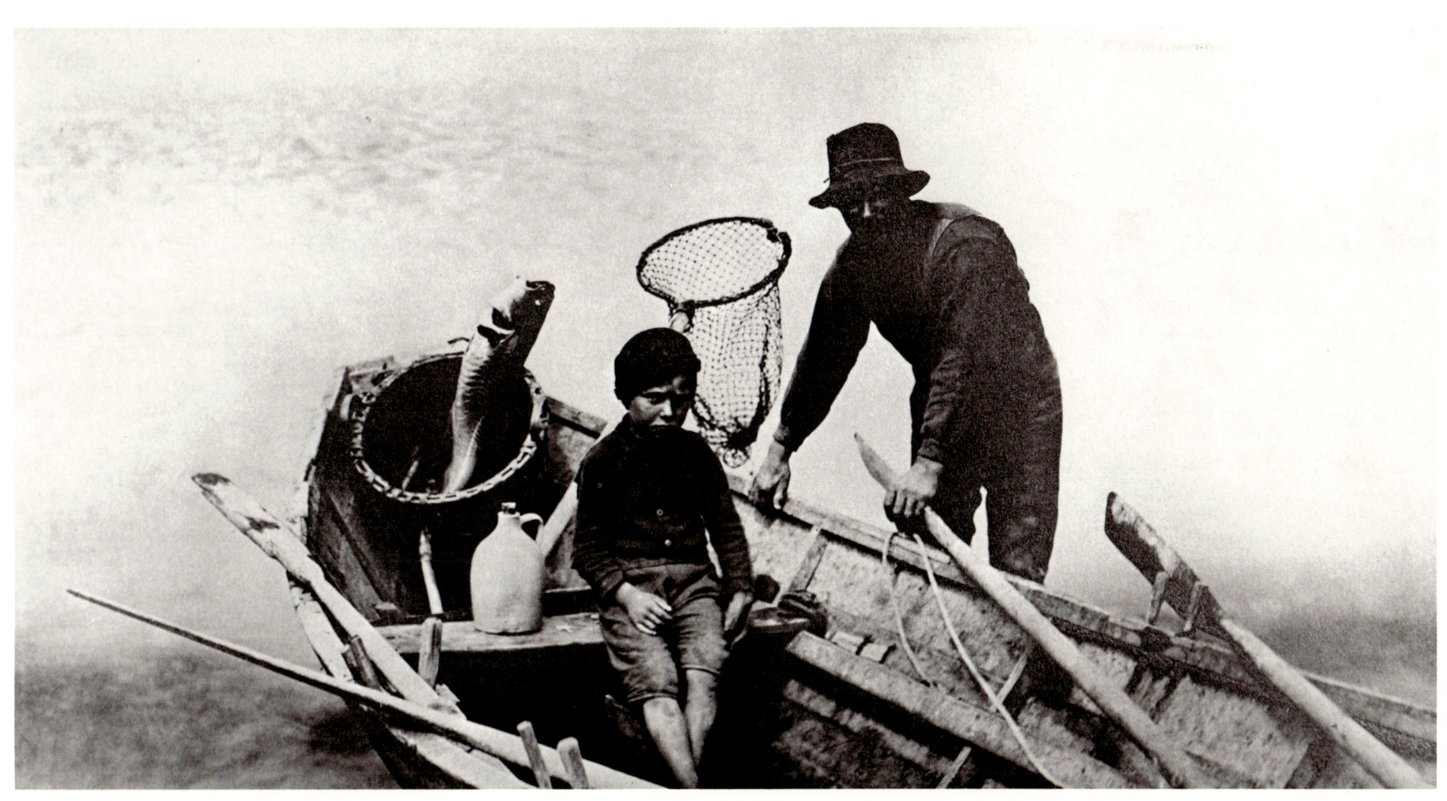

57. *Fred and Herbert Wallace*

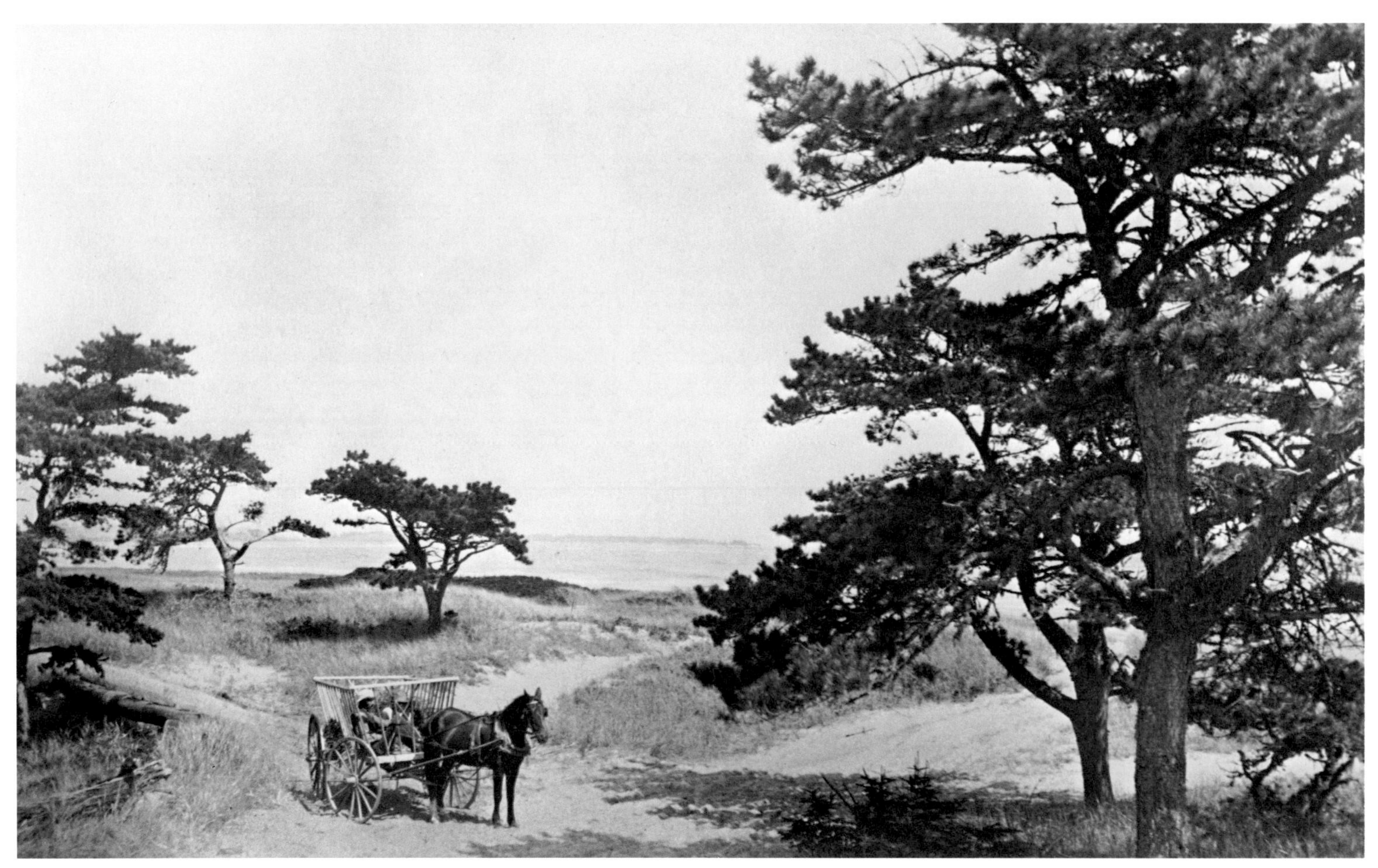

58. Near The Percy Cottage—Popham 1889

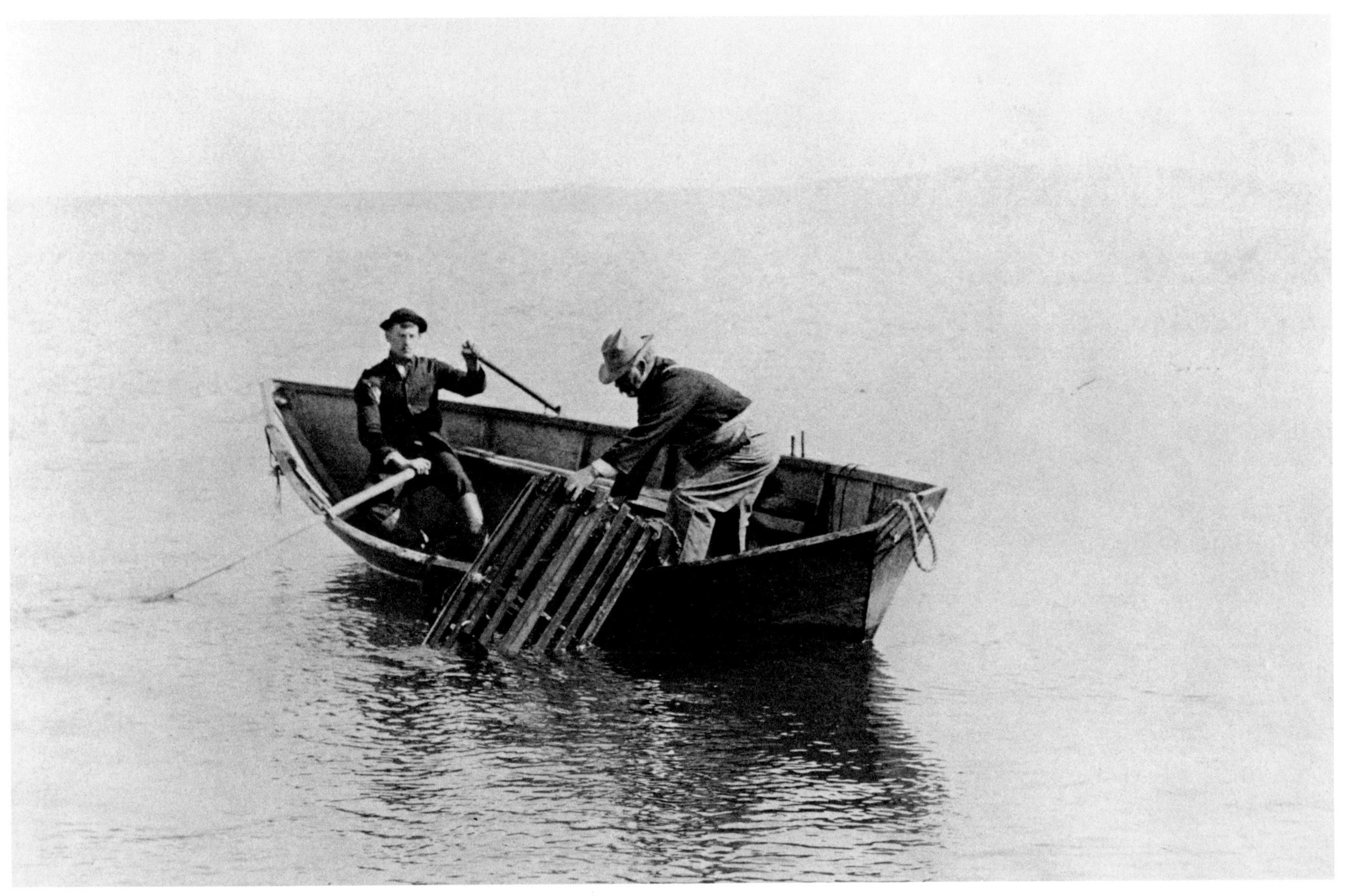

59. *Pulling Traps*

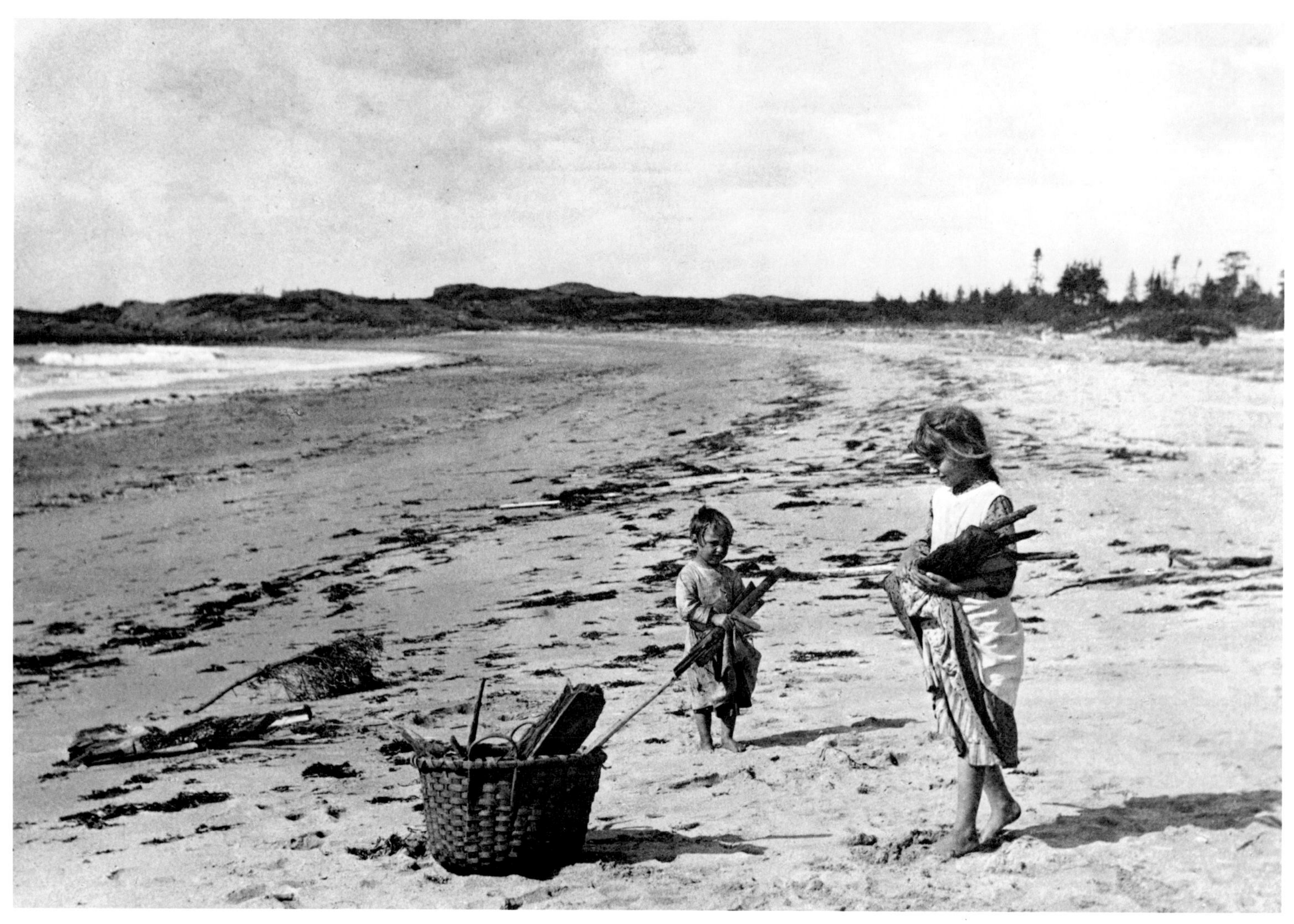

60. Untitled

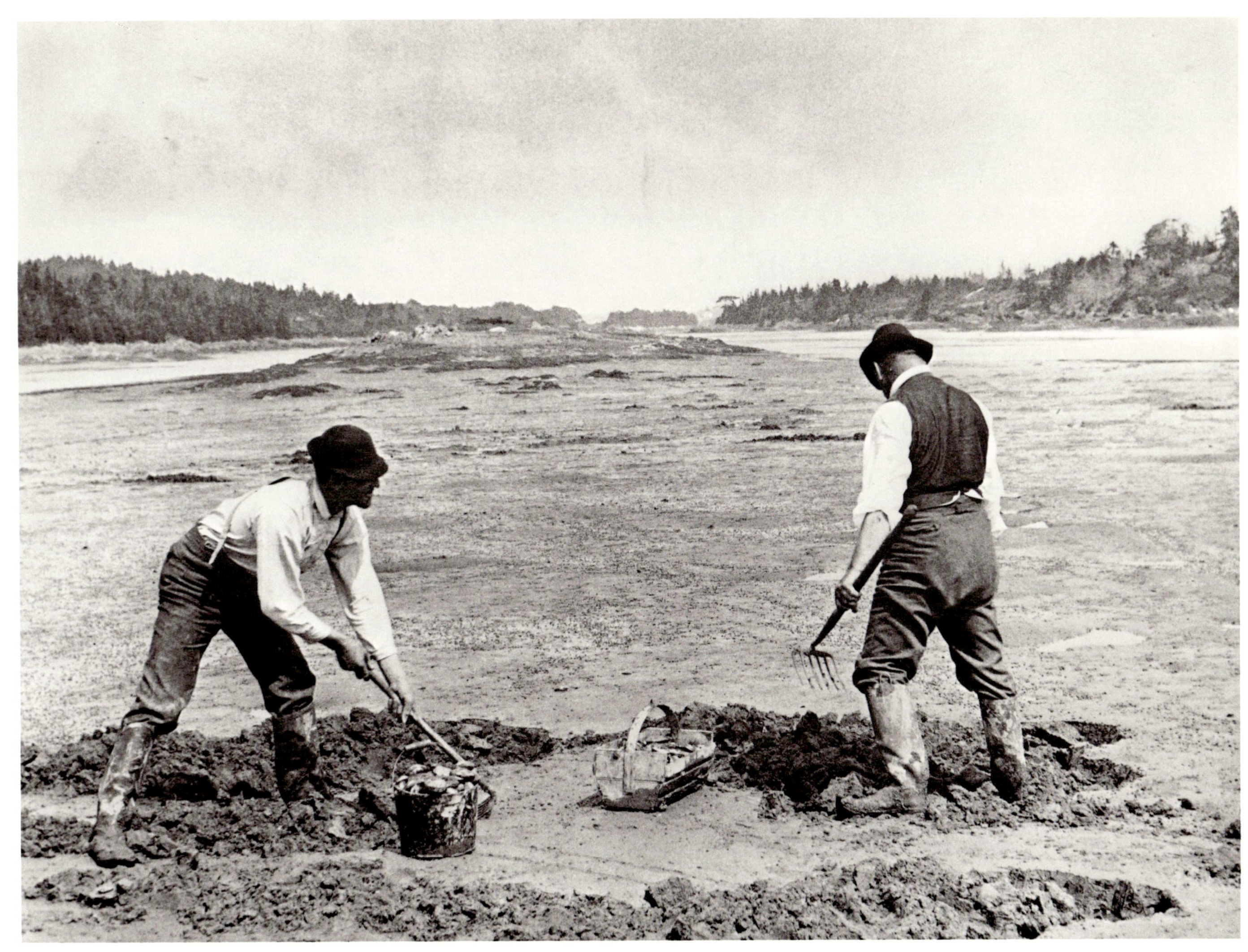

61. *The Clamdiggers*

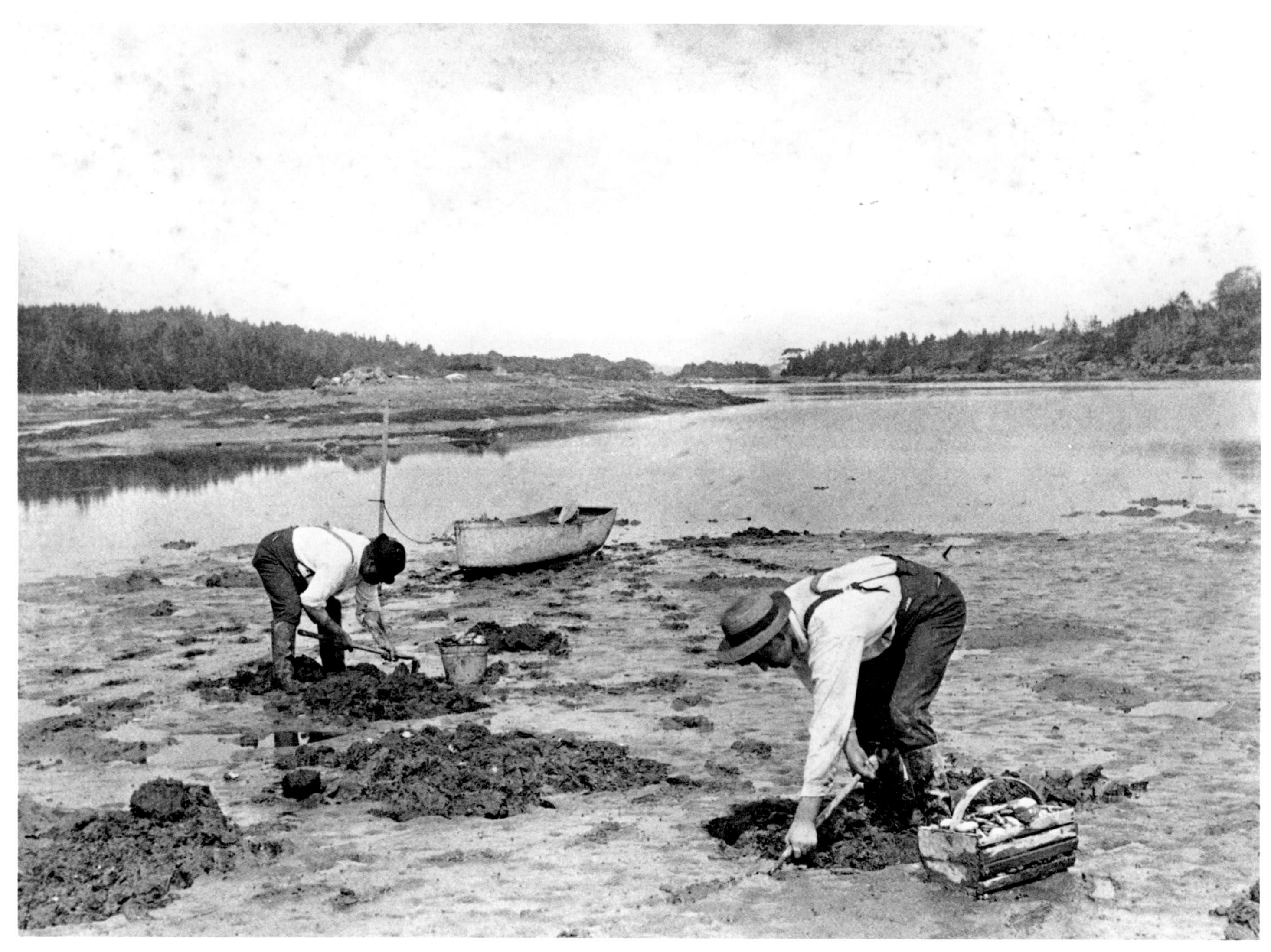

62. The Clamdiggers

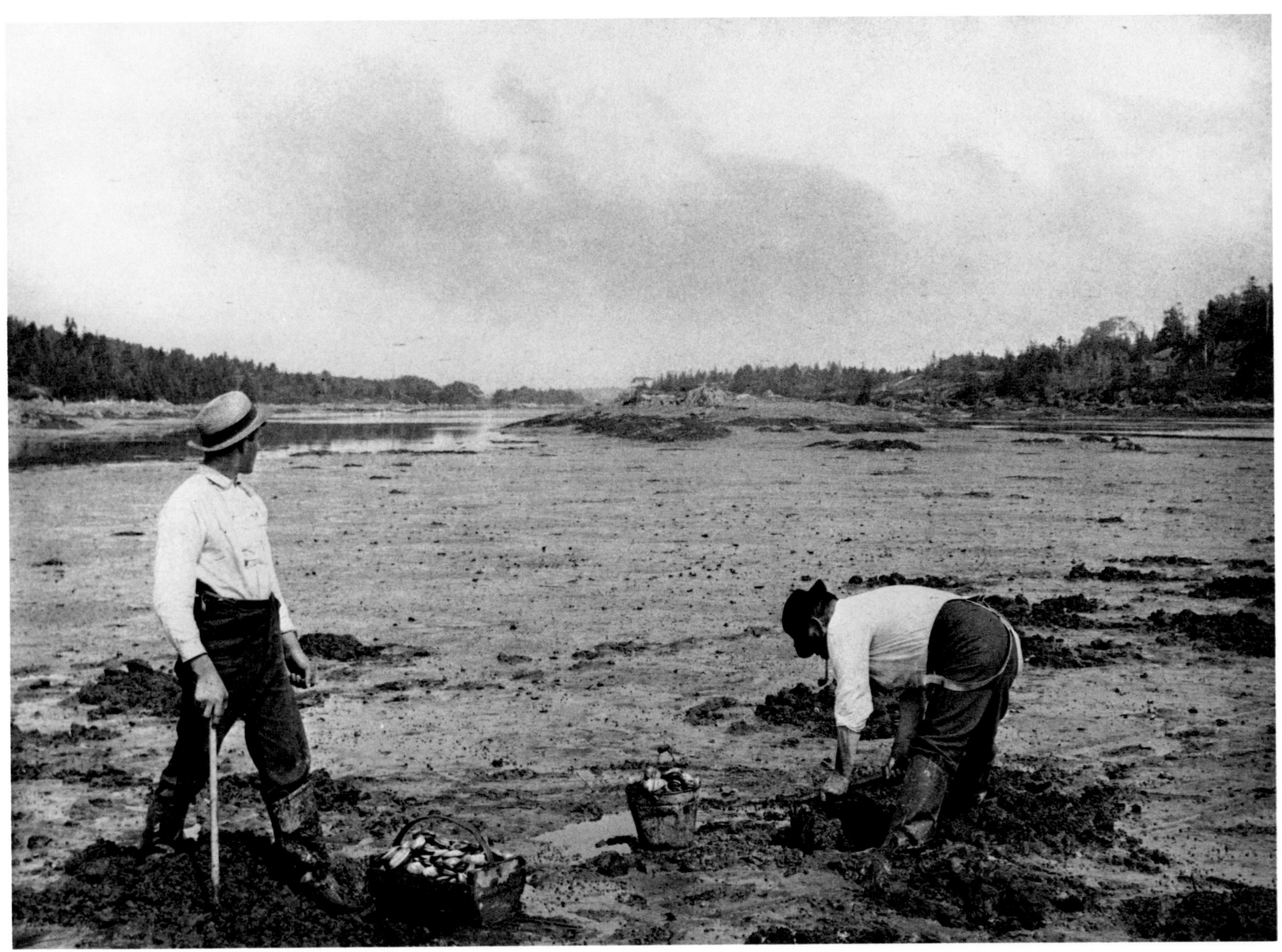

63. *The Clamdiggers*

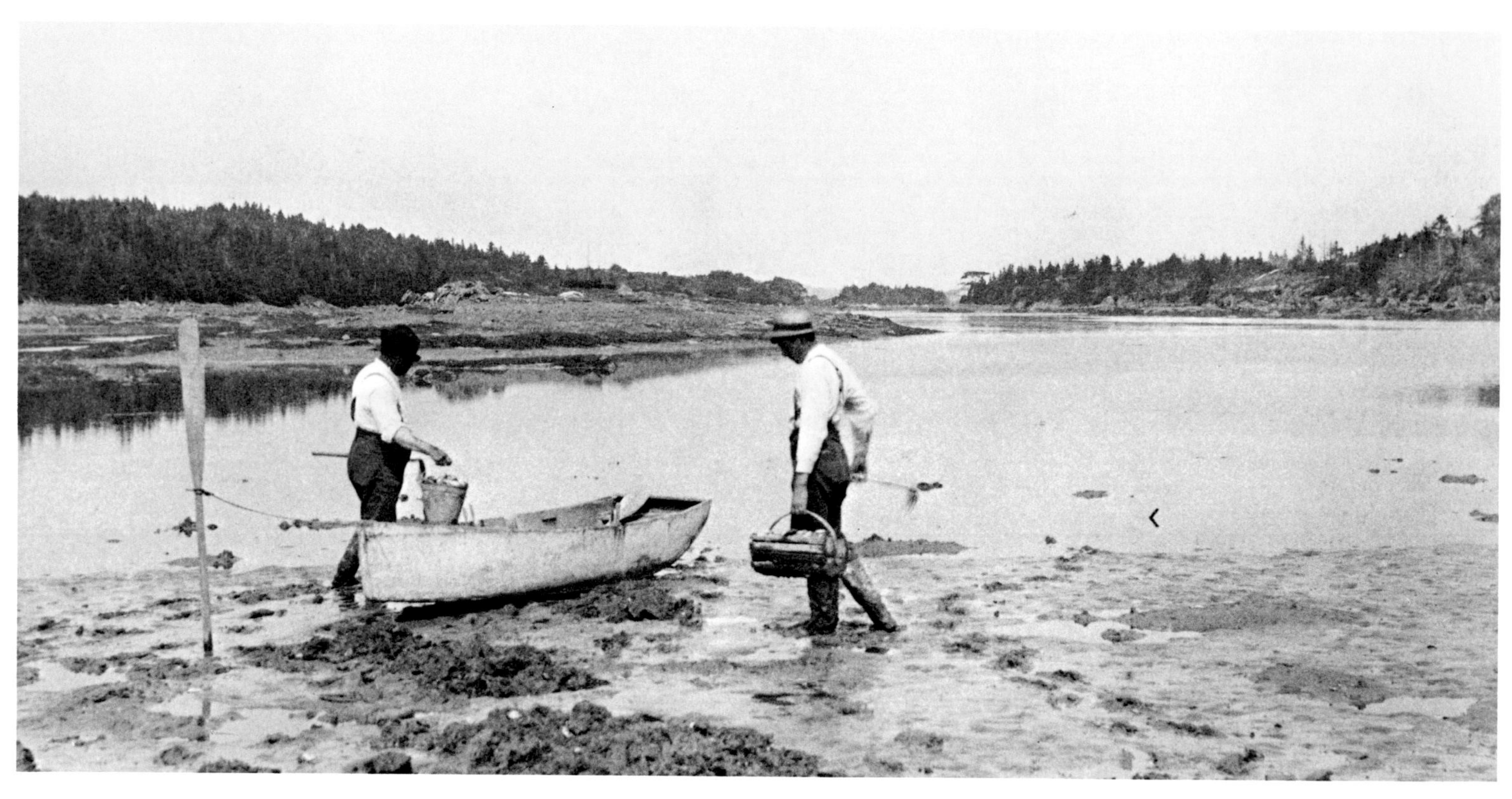

64. The Clamdiggers

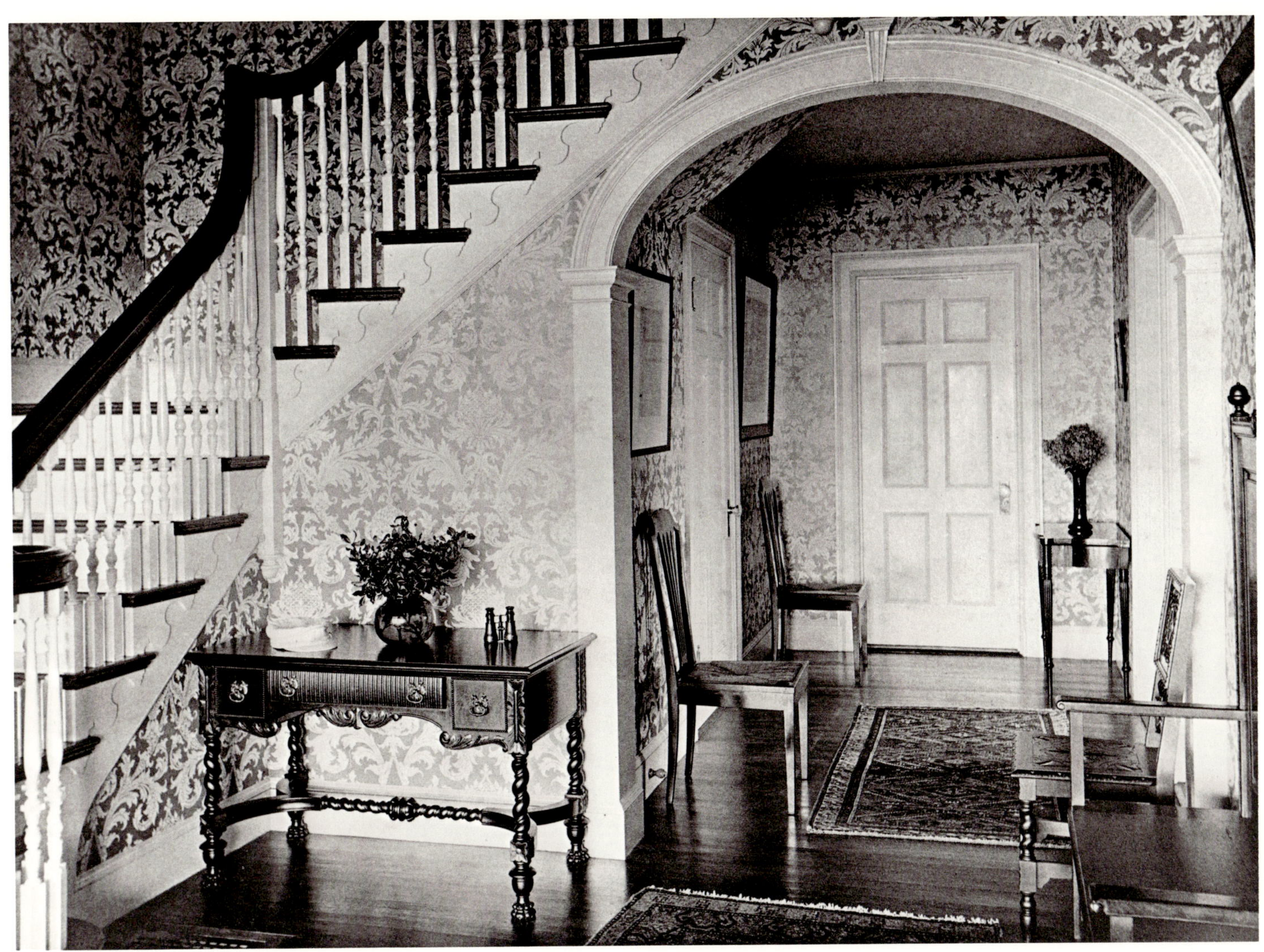

65. *Front hall*

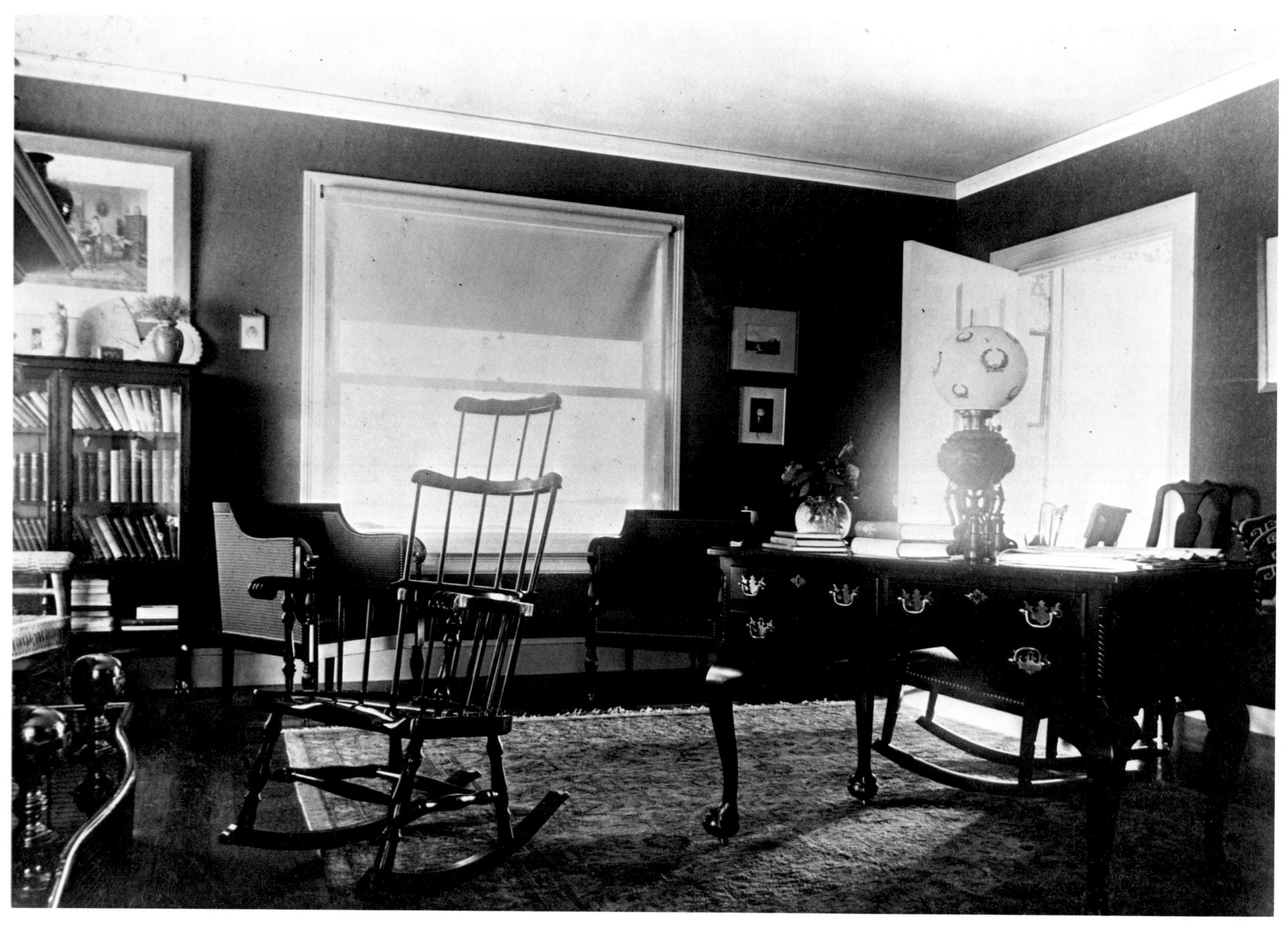

66. *Livingroom, looking southeast, 1899*

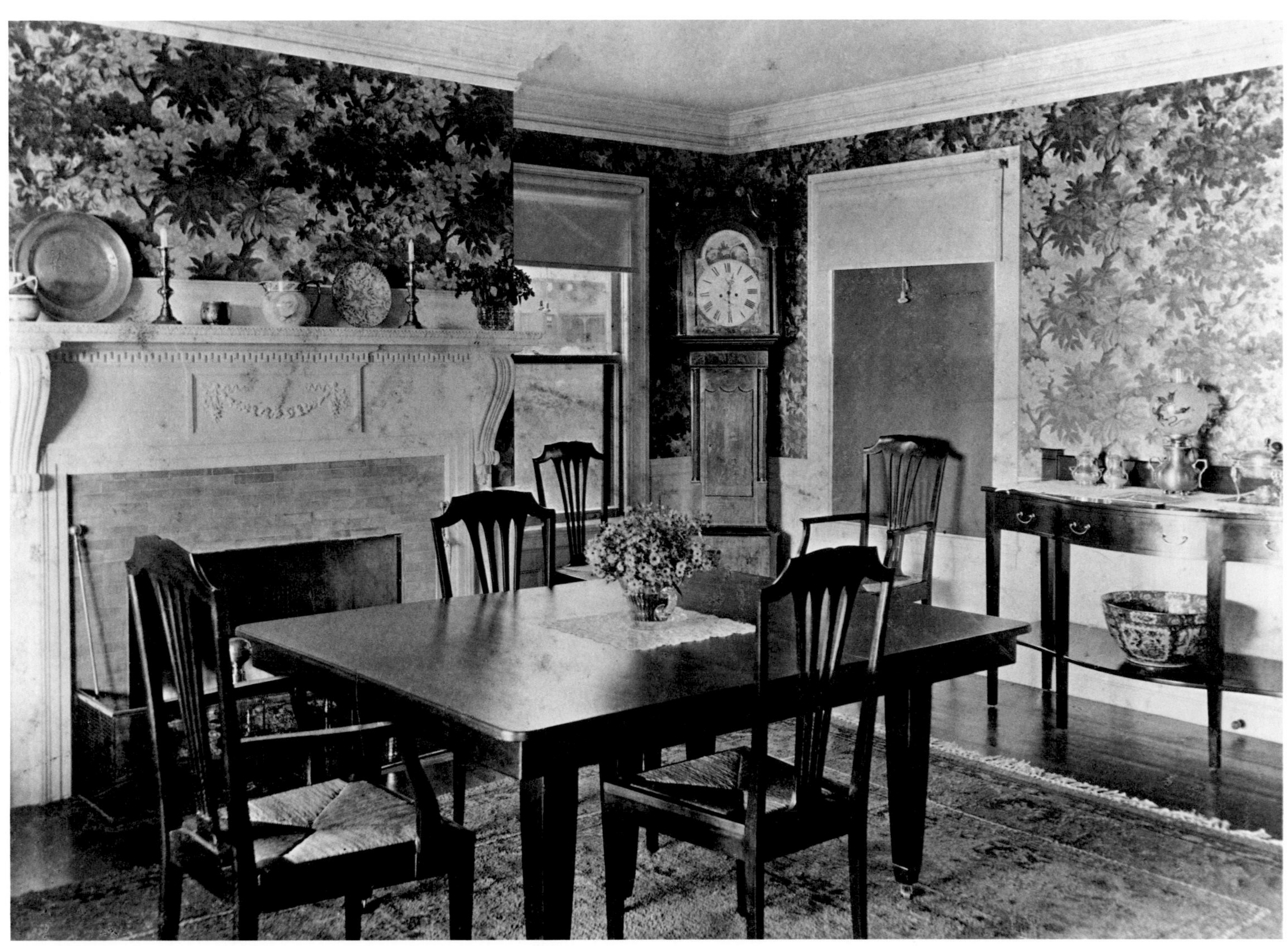

67. Diningroom

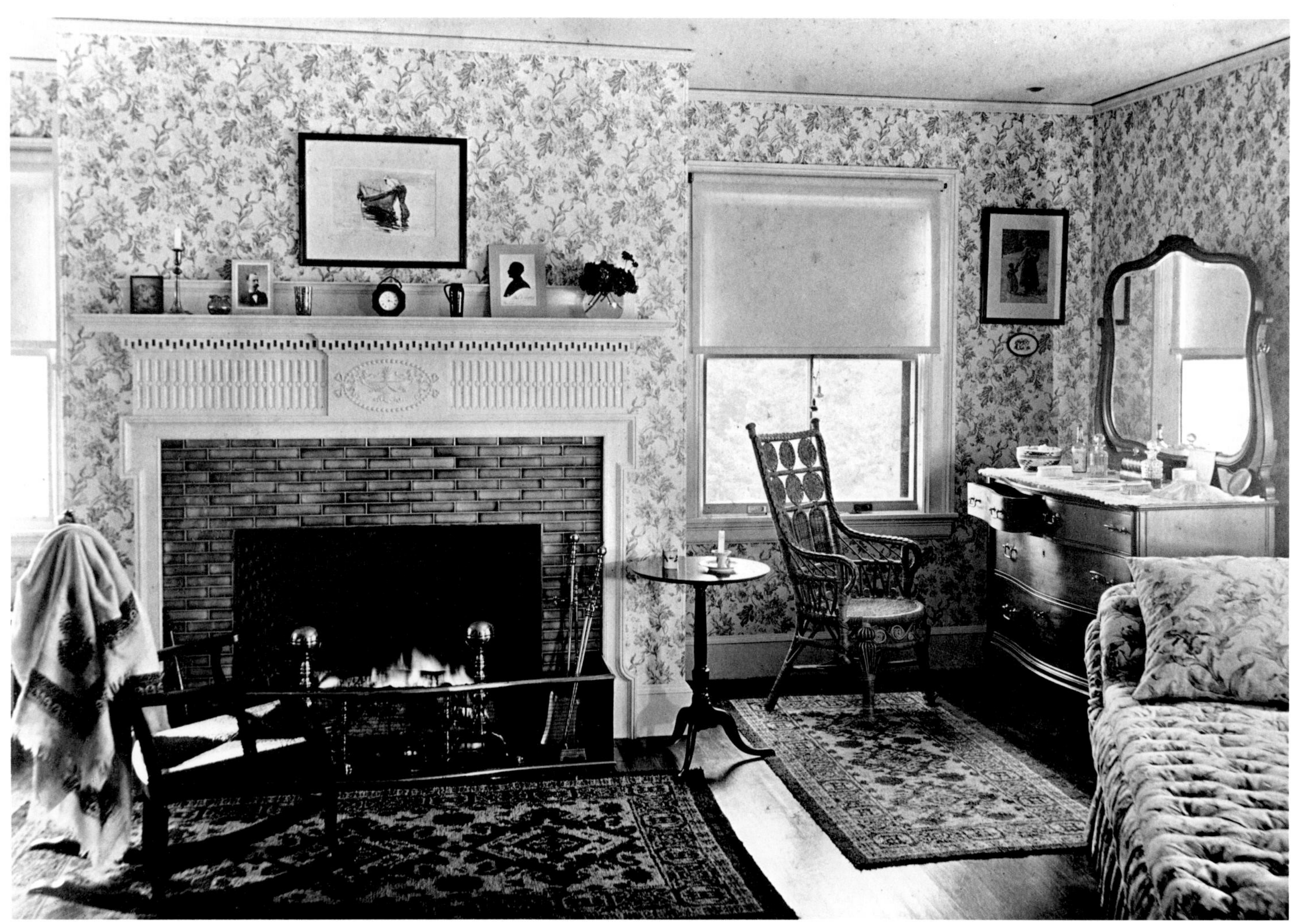

68. Untitled

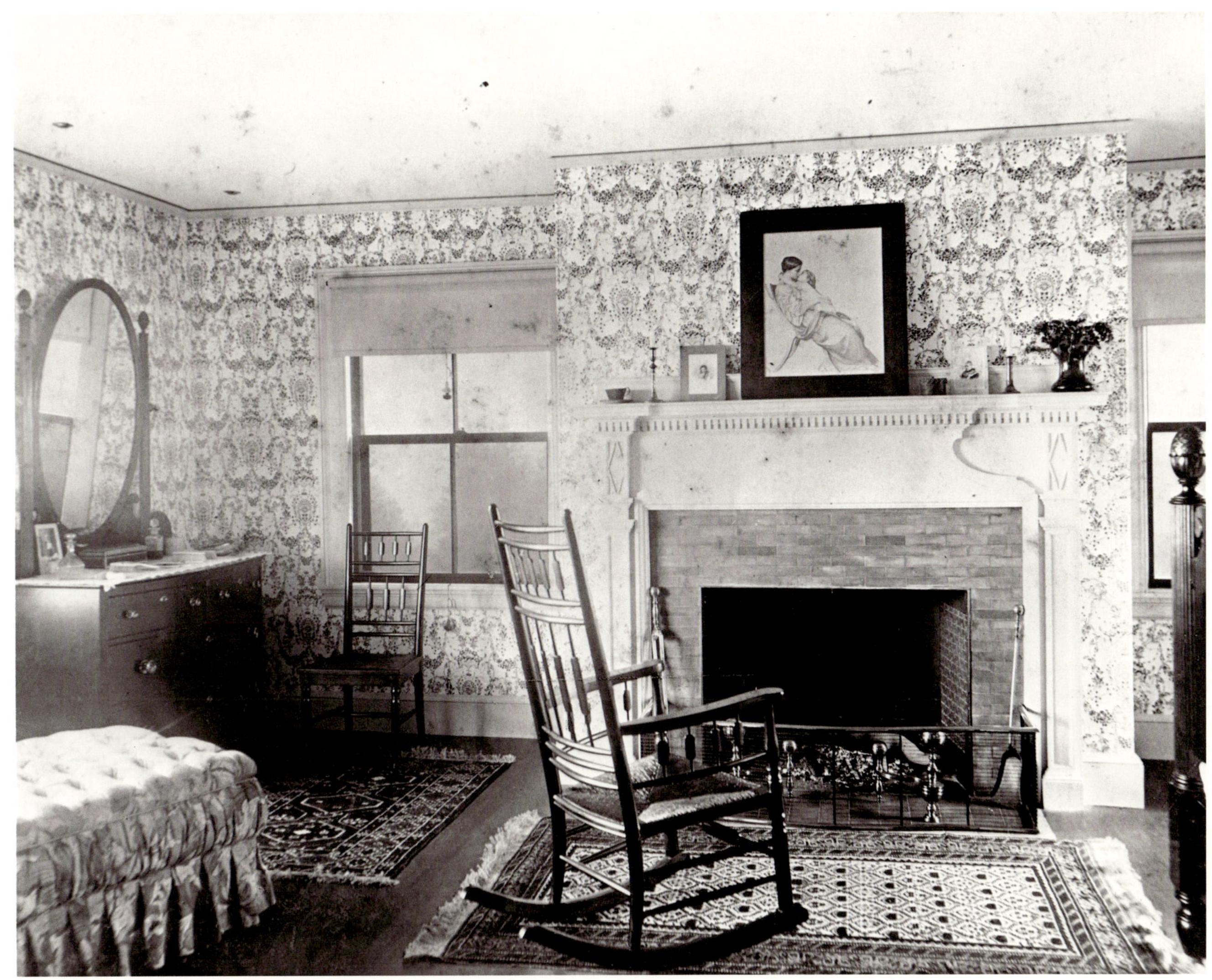

69. *Untitled*

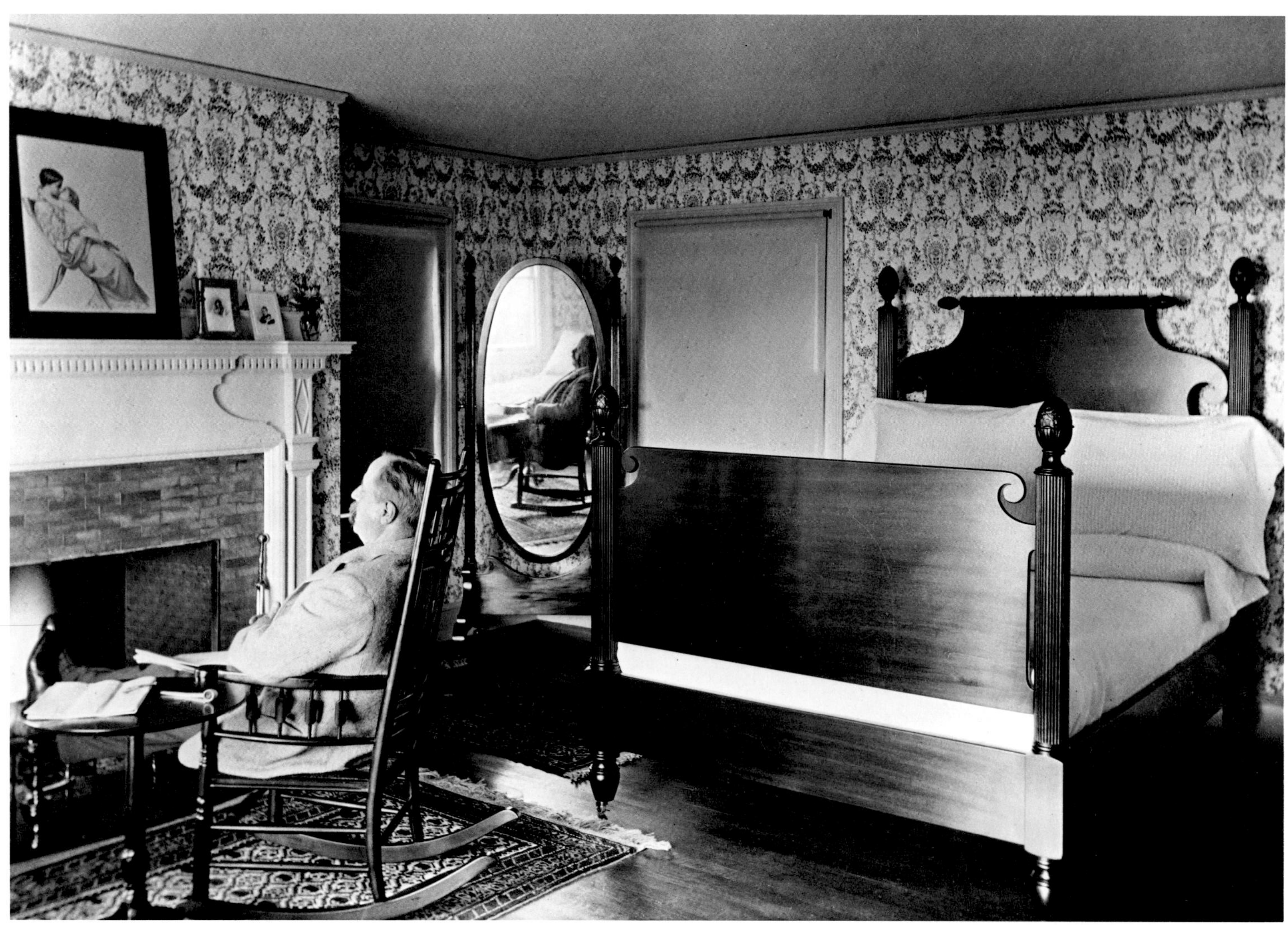

70. Untitled

Emma D. Sewall, 1836–1919

Chronology

1836	Born Sept. 17, Bath, Maine, to Charles Crooker and Rachel Sewall Crooker
1852	Mother, Rachel Sewall Crooker dies
1854–1855	Attended Ipswich Female Seminary, Ipswich, Massachusetts
1859	Married shipbuilder Arthur Sewall, Bath, Maine
1860	First son, Harold Marsh Sewall, born
1861	Second son, William Dunning Sewall, born
1864	Third son, Dummer Sewall, born (died at age two)
1860's–1870's	Summer trips with children kindle desire to create imagery
1884	Travels by railroad in United States and starts experimenting with photography (using dry-plate method)
1880's	Joins Postal Photographic Club, Fitchburg, Massachusetts
1894	Joins Boston Camera Club; receives two Postal Photographic Club first prizes for *On the Marshes* and *The Mowers*
1895	Receives three Boston Camera Club awards: first prize for most artistic merit for *Unloading Marsh Hay*; first prize for technical merit for *An Afternoon in February*; and the diploma for greatest general excellence. Four photographs hang in Paris at the Photo-Club of Paris: *The Clam Diggers, Fording the River, Small Farmhouse-interior,* and *Feeding the Hens*
1896	Receives Boston Camera Club first prize for *Harvest Time, Indian Summer, Autumn Ploughing, Study for Miss Wilkins*, and *The Village Blacksmith* Husband Arthur nominated for vice president at

	Democratic Convention, Chicago; Bryan and Sewall defeated by McKinley and Hobart after bitter partisan treatment by press
1897	Received Boston Camera Club award for best figure composition for *The Search* and *Village Blacksmith*
1898	Receives Boston Camera Club award (sterling silver bowl) for Illustrated Subject Competion for *When the Day's Work is Done*
	Receives Photo-Club of Paris award (silver-plated medal of honor) for *When the Day's Work is Done*
1899	Small Point summer home, The Dunes completed
	Alice Cutler, niece/companion of sixteen years, dies
1900	Arthur Sewall, husband, dies
	In mourning over loss of husband and niece, becomes reclusive, spending all but the coldest months at The Dunes
1905	Completes lyrical folklore history of Small Point area, *The Rivers and Marshes of Small Point* (published posthumously)
1906–1919	Continues reclusive life-style with emphasis on intellectual search
1919	Dies in her sleep, September 29, Small Point, Maine

Technical Information

The majority of Emma's photographs were taken with a mahogany Scovill field camera, manufactured by the Scovill Company in Waterbury, Connecticut from the 1880's through the 1890's. A common camera for its day, the Scovill used dry glass plates approximately 5 x 7″ in size for which she had five wooden holders.

Her other camera (pictured on page 8) is in pristine condition, but has no label on the camera body. Also made of mahogany, this camera closely fits the description of a camera made by the American Optical Company in New York listed in the 1891 *Illustrated Catalogue of Photographic Equipments and Materials for Amateurs*: "Flammang's Patent Revolving Back Camera—c1886. Tailboard style view camera, with patent revolving and tilting back. Mahogany body with brass fittings. Tapered bellows, rising front. Usually found in 5 x 7″ and 6½ x 8½″ sizes. $150–175."

The lens on this camera is still intact. It is a Prosch Triplex lens, manufactured between 1889 and 1895 and was the top of the line among the Prosch lenses. For this camera, Emma had six wooden glass plate holders (6 x 8″ format), embossed with "American Optical Company, Patent May 15, 1883," and stored in a wooden carrying case.

On most of her glass plate holders, there are notes written in chalk indicating subject matter and exposure times which range from seven minutes to one and one quarter hours for the interior shots of The Dunes. The notations indicate that she favored small f-stop settings and long exposure times. Helmut Gernsheim, in his *The History of Photography 1685–1914*, writes that exposures with people as subjects were in the range of 1/125th to four seconds during the time Emma was taking photographs. When artificial light was used, it was a magnesium flash with very harsh effects, resulting in a high contrast image. However, none of Emma's notes refer to the use of flash, so it is probable that she tended towards longer exposures and natural light, even in her photographs of people.

From her glass plates, Emma made platinum prints, which were popular from 1873 to 1920. In *A Guide to Early Photographic Processes*, Brian Coe and Mark Haworth-Booth write, "platinum prints were invented by William Willis in 1873. The materials for the process were marketed from 1879. Plain paper containing light sensitive iron salts, (but no silver), and a platinum compound was exposed in contact with a negative (glass plate) to daylight. The exposed print was developed in a solution of potassium oxalate, finely divided platinum metal being deposited in the paper to form the image. The finely divided platinum was intensely black, and the platinum print shows characteristic rich blacks, and completely neutral, almost silvery-grey mid tones. By developing the print in a hot developer a warmer, almost sepia platinum image was produced."

Emma titled many of her photographs but only sometimes identified her subjects by name. A photo album of Emma's prints provided the main source from which I found names to her subjects. It is possible that some of her subjects were employed by the Sewalls, but I have no verification of this. Generally, it is not known on what basis she chose her subjects.

I made my prints by photographing the unframed originals with a Polaroid MP-4 copy camera, using 4 x 5″ Kodak Plus-X film and by making contact prints from some of her glass plates. I printed my negatives and the plates on Agfa Brovira 111, numbers 2 and 3, and Agfa Portriga Rapid 111, numbers 2 and 3 depending on the contrast of the negative or glass plate. I developed the prints in Kodak Dektol developer diluted 1 : 2 and I selinium toned the Brovira prints to achieve warmer blacks.

Photographic Index of Plates

1. *When The Day's Work Is Done* Contact print from glass plate. Exhibited in 1898 at Boston Camera Club: awarded sterling silver bowl for Illustrated Subject Competition. Exhibited in 1898 at Photo-Club of Paris: awarded silver plated Medal of Honor.
2. Untitled. Woman quilting.
3. *The Search* Exhibited in 1897 at Boston Camera Club: award for Best Figure Composition.
4. *Mrs. Young*
5. *Study for Miss Wilkins* Exhibited in 1896 at Boston Camera Club: award for Most Artistic Merit.
6. *Mrs. Coffee—Small Point*
7. Untitled. Woman knitting by window. Contact print from glass plate. 1894 calendar indicates Emma probably exhibited this photograph in 1895 at the Boston Camera Club: awarded the "prize for the greatest general excellence for compositions including landscapes, old-fashioned New England interiors, sea views, and genre subjects indoors and in the open air."
8. *The Sleeping Grandmother*
9. *Fairbanks Homestead* Newspaper clipping on picture frame states: "June, 1903, Fairbanks Family Reunion—The twelth annual homecoming of the Fairbanks family of America will be held at the Fairbanks homestead, Dedham, Mass., August 21, 1903, morning and afternoon. This homestead is the original house, built in 1636, and is the oldest frame dwelling in New England. It has always been in the possession of the Fairbanks family."
10. *A Clearing Near Moosehead Lake*
11. *Old House At New Meadows—Built 1762*
12. *. . . corner of Pine and Washington Street* (Writing illegible.)
13. *Roger's House—Phippsburg 1887*
14. *The Cottage Door*
15. *Indian Summer—Near Topsham* Exhibited in 1896 at the Boston Camera Club: award for Most Artistic Merit.
16. *The Carriage Smith At Work—Harpswell Road 1888*

17. *The Village Blacksmith* Exhibited in 1896 at the Boston Camera Club: award for Most Artistic Merit. Exhibited in 1897 at the Boston Camera Club: award for Best Figure Composition.
18. *Home of the Country Carriage Smith—Harpswell Road 1888*
19. *Small Farmhouse Interior—1890* Probably among those prints exhibited in 1895 at the Boston Camera Club: awarded the "prize for greatest general excellence for compositions including landscapes, old-fashioned New England interiors, sea views, and genre subjects indoors and in the open air." Exhibited 1895 at the Photo-Club of Paris.
20. *Going To Market*
21. *The Lobsterman*
22. *The Garret—Sewall's Mills*
23. *Blueberry Pickers*
24. *Feeding The Hens* Exhibited in 1895 at the Boston Camera Club: awarded the "prize for greatest general excellence. . ." Exhibited in 1895 at the Photo-Club of Paris.
25. Untitled. Farmer collecting eggs.
26. Untitled. Churning butter.
27. *Blueberry Pickers*
28. *Autumn Ploughing* Exhibited in 1896 at the Boston Camera Club: awarded Prize for Most Artistic Merit.
29. *Harvest Time* Exhibited in 1896 at the Boston Camera Club: award for Most Artistic Merit.
30. Untitled. Two girls on their way to pick blueberries.
31. *Whetting The Scythe* Mr. William Coffee with scythe, which was used on marshland that was too wet for an oxen cart.
32. *Unloading Marsh Hay* Exhibited in 1895 at the Boston Camera Club: award for Most Artistic Merit.
33. *Cutting Thatch* Jimmie Thompson with scythe on Wyman marshland, near Burying Hill. Sprague River in background.
34. *Just Unloaded*
35. *Poling Hay—A Foggy Day On The Marshes* Jimmie Thompson on right.
36. Untitled. Arthur Sewall at far right.

37. *The Mowers* Waitstill Wallace eating apple. Exhibited in 1894 at Postal Photographic Club (probably in a circulating exhibition book), Fitchburg, Massachusetts: awarded First Prize.

38. *On The Marshes* Exhibited in 1894 at Postal Photographic Club, Fitchburg, Massachusetts.

39. *Fording The River* Probably exhibited in 1895 at the Boston Camera Club: award for greatest general excellence. Exhibited in 1895 at the Photo-Club of Paris.

40. Untitled. Man with scythe, with back to camera.

41. *Herbert Wallace In His Father's Fish House*

42. *Pulling Traps*

43. *Alliquippa Harbor—Small Point*

44. *Small Point* Fred Wallace holding up net.

45. *Salting Bait—Small Point 1888*

46. *Anderson Cottage—Small Point 1888*

47. *End Of The Bluff—Small Point* Also known as *Ice Box Bend.*

48. *The Young Boatman*

49. *In Alliquippa Harbor* Back of print is inscribed, "For my grandson, Arthur Sewall 2nd, from E. D. S." The schooner is the *Lillie Alice*, a scow schooner with a crew of one, fifty-one and a half feet registered length, used as a cargo vessel and built in 1890 in Harpswell at Clark's Cove. It's homeport was Portland. (Information courtesy of the Maine Maritime Museum).

50. *Cleaning Fish* Near Johnson's Pound, Small Point.

51. *Road To Johnson's Pound—Small Point 1889*

52. *Playing In The Water*

53. *Mending The Net*

54. *Rocky Inlet—Small Point, West Side, 1889*

55. *Gathering Driftwood—Head Beach, Small Point*

56. Untitled. Back Bay, looking north, Small Point.

57. *Fred and Herbert Wallace*

58. *Near The Percy Cottage—Popham 1889*

59. *Pulling Traps*

60. Untitled. Two girls collecting driftwood.

61. *The Clamdiggers* Back of picture frame says 1895. Probably

exhibited in 1895 at the Boston Camera Club. Exhibited in 1895 at the Photo-Club of Paris, and reproduced in their exhibition catalogue, entitled *Deuxieme Exposition d' Art Photographique Paris 1895*.

62. *The Clamdiggers* Back of frame says 1895.
63. *The Clamdiggers*
64. *The Clamdiggers*
65. *Front hall*
66. *Livingroom* Looking southeast, 1899.
67. *Diningroom*
68. Untitled. Bedroom.
69. Untitled. Bedroom.
70. Untitled. Arthur relaxing in bedroom at The Dunes, 1899.

Select Bibliography

Books

Abbott, Berenice. *The World of Atget.* New York: Horizon Press, 1964.

Ascher, Carol; Louise DeSalvo and Sara Ruddick, eds. *Between Women.* Boston: Beacon Press, 1984.

Baker, William Avery. *A Maritime History of Bath, Maine and the Kennebec River Region.* 2 vols. Bath, Maine: Marine Research Society of Bath, 1973.

Berger, John. *About Looking.* New York: Pantheon Books, 1980.

Bunnell, Peter C., ed. *A Photographic Vision: Pictorial Photography 1889–1923.* Salt Lake City: Peregrine Smith, Inc., 1980.

Coe, Brian, and Mark Haworth-Booth. *A Guide to Early Photographic Processes.* London: Victoria & Albert Museum, 1983.

Frank, Waldo; Lewis Mumford, Dorothy Norman, Paul Rosenfeld, and Harold Rugg. *America & Alfred Stieglitz: A Collective Portrait.* New York: Literary Guild, 1934.

Goldberg, Natalie. *Writing Down The Bones: Freeing the Writer Within.* Boston: Shambhala, 1986.

Green, Jonathan, ed. *Camera Work: A Critical Anthology.* New York: Aperture, 1973.

Hennessy, Mark W. *Sewall Ships of Steel.* Augusta, Maine: The Kennebec Journal Press, 1937.

Homer, William Innes. *Alfred Stieglitz and the American Avant-garde.* Boston: New York Graphic Society, 1977.

Jussim, Estelle. *Slave To Beauty: The Eccentric Life & Career of F. Holland Day Photographer & Publisher.* Boston: David R. Godine, 1981.

Norman, Dorothy. *Alfred Stieglitz: An American Seer.* New York: Random House, 1973.

Owen, Henry Wilson. *The Edward Clarence Plummer History of Bath, Maine.* Bath, Maine: Times Company, 1936.

Peladeau, Marius B. *Chansonetta: The Life and Photographs of Chansonetta Stanley Emmons 1858–1937*. Waldoboro, Maine: Maine Antique Digest, 1977. Distributed by Morgan & Morgan, Inc., 145 Palisade St., Dobbs Ferry, New York 10522.

Stegner, Wallace. *Angle of Repose*. Garden City, New York: Doubleday, 1971.

Sternburg, Janet, ed. *The Writer On Her Work*. New York: W. W. Norton & Company, 1980.

Theroux, Paul. *Picture Palace*. Boston: Houghton Mifflin, 1978.

Periodicals, Museum Catalogues and Unpublished Material

American Amateur Photographer, vols. 7, 10.

Boston Camera Club exhibition catalogs, 1895–1900. Boston Athenaeum, Boston.

Culture and Record. Nineteenth century photographs from the University of New Mexico Art Museum Catalog #14. Albuquerque: University of New Mexico, 1984.

D'Art Photographique Deuxieme Exposition. Paris: Photo-Club de Paris, 1895.

Hill, Mary Pelham. "Sewall Genealogy." Commissioned by Harold Marsh Sewall, 1921.

Sewall, Emma D. "Diary calendar." Three hundred sixty-five quotations presented to William D. Sewall in calendar form, 1905.

Sewall, Emma D. *The Great Political Campaign of '96 Volume I*. Unpublished book containing national and international press documentation of Bryan-Sewall Presidential campaign, 1896.

White, Maynard Presley, Jr. "Clarence H. White: A Personal Portrait." Doctoral thesis, University of Delaware, 1975.